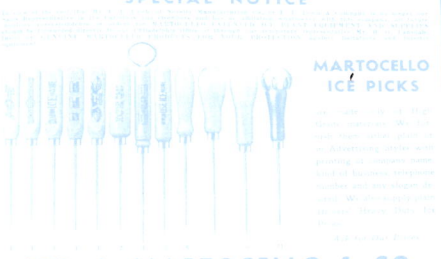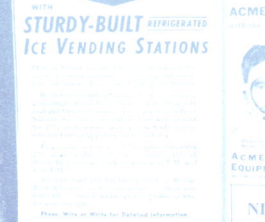

COOLING THE SOUTH

THE BLOCK ICE ERA

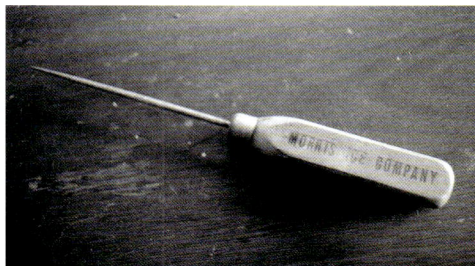

elli morris

1875-1975

Foreword by Curtis Wilkie

Elli Morris

©Elli Morris. All rights reserved.
No part of this book may be reproduced or transmitted in any form without the written permission of the publisher.
Refrigeration photos are used by permission.
Published by Wackophoto
P.O. Box 14843
Richmond, VA 23221
www.wackophoto.com
Library of Congress Control Number: 2007935975
ISBN# 978-0-9798532-0-3
Printed in China by Everbest Printing Co. through Four Colour Imports, Ltd., Louisville, Kentucky.
Written and photographed by Elli Morris.
Image scanning by Digital Image Group.
Design by Heidi Flynn Barnett, Flynn Design.

Table of Contents

Dedication	5
Acknowledgments	6
Foreword by Curtis Wilkie	8
The Family Business	12
Community Involvement	24
The Gorrie Facts	36
Ice and Iron	42
Three Hundred Pound Cakes!	54
Chip Off the Old Block	62
Hometown Memories	68
Unsung Hero	78
The Melt Down	86
Frozen Assets	94
Bibliography	106

Ice tongs, Pete Stack collection.

Dedication

My uncle Hebron's stories about the "Strawberry Special" train carrying its precious cargo from Louisiana up to Chicago are really the inspiration for this book. Block ice, which kept the berries from spoiling, was the hero in the stories. A true iceman himself, Hebron's engaging accounts of his peers working, being strong and having a good time were all the better in his slow, Southern drawl and I eagerly listened whenever I returned home to Jackson, Mississippi where our family had an icehouse.

While on the "trail of the abandoned ice plants," as Hebron so aptly named this undertaking, I relied on his expertise at every step. He furnished lists of contacts from his time in business, set up appointments with acquaintances and unearthed old photographs, documents and bookkeeping records that fueled my fire to be an ice chronicler at large. He plied my boyfriend and me with great food, great conversation and memorable outings to remote locals in Mississippi. Hebron reviewed every version of the manuscript, and there were quite a few, for technical accuracy, making numerous corrections and sending typed notes detailing important omitted facts. He was indispensable in creating my interest in ice, explaining the mechanics of the machinery and financially supporting my efforts. Without his help, I would never have been able to successfully document that extraordinary moment in time, the block ice era.

Two weeks after I opened a savings account as seed money for this project I went on my first date with Ryan Norton. For the next three years, he unrelentingly supported me and had more faith in me than I knew any human could. He not only let me talk *ad nauseam* about ice, but he offered advice and input, constantly impressing me that he was actually listening, not just being an obliging boyfriend.

After our joint trip to Mississippi in August, Ryan's introduction to the Deep South, I returned to my darkroom and developed the first round of film only to find I had underexposed the shots. I fell to my hands and knees and started wailing in deep sobs, banging my head on the floor as I gasped for air. Ryan dismissed my fears without batting an eye. Nonchalantly, he walked into the darkroom, looked at my immense failures and said, "I could print something like this when I was in high school. What's your problem?" I caught my breath, stoop up, looked at the negatives with him by my side and vaguely smiled at him. He gave me a lasting gift that afternoon; perfectionism had to go.

When I received a letter from a publisher who was interested in the manuscript, Ryan and I had a grand time joyfully celebrating that momentary success. He left me a voicemail saying "And I'm not surprised in the least! It's just the payoff on a whole lot of blood, sweat and tears, pain, dedication and devotion." I still have that message on my machine. Ryan was killed on his beloved motorcycle two weeks after that night of public affirmation. In my grief, I polished up the manuscript, sent it off to the publisher and cried my eyes out at the loss of my best friend, lover, and supporter. I remain eternally grateful for Ryan's steadfast belief in me and his undying love.

Acknowledgments

The backbone of this book is the first-hand accounts of the men and women who created and enjoyed the world's first means of artificial coolness. Their knowledge put flesh on the skeletons of information I found at my family's shut-down ice plant, facilitating my efforts to bring to life the bygone era of block ice.

To all the ice plant owners and workers, thank you for letting me interrupt your business during the summer, only the busiest time of year, and for so graciously sharing your incredible stories about life at a working block ice plant: Anderson Peters, Ben Fulgham, Billy Ross Brown, Buddy Duke, Charles Bridges, Charlie Watson, Chris Fortner, Dan Jones, David Bush, David Gautier, David Hildebrandt, David Romig, Duey Carter, Gerard Montz, James Barr, Jim Weaver, John Yopp, Kathy Barth, Kenny Cristina, Louis Robertson, Jr., Mary Cronley and the entire gang at *Refrigeration*, the illusive Mr. Eppy, Nathaniel Sandifer, Pete Stack, Raymond "Yank" Harris, Rob Davis, Rob Neal, Robert Cristina, Steve Quinlivan, Tommy Polk, W.C. Sonny Fortner, Jr. and Walter G. Ribeiro, Sr.

To all the interviewees, your memories are treasures for those of us who can only imagine the block ice era. More than one hundred people offered me some worthwhile tidbit of information about life with big blocks of ice. To family members, friends of friends, all the strangers I accosted on the streets of small towns and anyone over the age of fifty who was in my presence, thank you for freely sharing your stories and for the engaging conversations about ice.

To all of you who let Ryan and me crash at your house, willingly fed us and in general supported this endeavor in any way, I would never have left home without you: Alice and Morris Alexander, Aunt Terry and Dave, Brandi Holley, "Britt" Brittney, Charles and Margaret Tribble, Clara Schleh, Connie and Gary White, Corinne and Chuck Sampson, Dean Alexander, Debby Reinke, Elaine Pruitt and her girls Vera Grace and Carisa, the Fish House Restaurant staff and customers, Greta Wharton, Jeff Saxman for giving me a great deal on my first 4x5 camera, Jennifer Larson, John Larus of Phototech who developed all my film without cross-processing a single sheet or roll, Joy and Ted Cleary and their beautiful baby Ella, Kelvin Andrews, Key Ivy, Kristen and Jason Sneed who let Ryan and me take over their side yard with our camper for several months, Lynn Holder, Mabel Rogers who is the best cook in the state of Mississippi, Marianne Hill and her daughter Rosie Hill, Michael Van Hecke for lovingly coming to Ryan's funeral, the entire Nixon family, the Octogenarians at Mexico Beach: Helen LaPlante, Mary Nolan and Mid "Pinky" Behmke, the Retirees at Rustic Sands which is the best RV campground in Florida, Rosie Gammell, Roy and Bonnie Norton, Shack Up Inn, Stephen and Marlo Carter Kirkpatrick, Sue Hiller, Taylor and Hannah Silver for just being ever-so cool, Thomas Scott who eventually paid the electricity bill at the darkroom, Tracey Lee who makes burning through money seem like a fun thing to do, and Walt Grayson.

Thank you to those of you who believed in this project with your dollars, making donations or buying an advance copy of the book—sometimes three years in advance. Who knew it would take so long to document the undocumented history of a by-gone era?! Thank you Baird Green, Corinne and Chuck Sampson, Hebron Morris, Jere Kittle who not only gave cash but contributed an exquisite web site for this project, Jessica Ledbetter and Ranee Barsanti, John Hebron Moore, Marcee and Jay Silver for their multiple donations, Ridgeway Lane and Walt Ribeiro.

To all the editors who read the many versions of the manuscript, especially to those of you who read the disjointed ones and still encouraged me with notes and practical advice, I thank you for your skills and kindness: Donna Gregory, Dotty Rilee, Faye and Merwin Van Hecke who rose to the desperate call of editing the book NOW so I could get it off to a prospective publisher, Hebron Morris, Lynn Vandenesse, and Marlo Carter Kirkpatrick.

To the most talented, honest and caring graphic artist, Heidi Barnett who is also a dear friend: I remain thrilled that you wanted to work on this project, that you put your magic touch to the pages of this book and that you told me the truth even when I really didn't want anything to do with another rewrite. Thank you for turning all my hard work into a beautiful and cohesive book.

To my dear friends who have listened to me whim, complain and go broke over this project: Becky Hord, Benjyman Pritchett, Carmen Martinez, Dotty Rilee, Jack Huber, Lori Valente, Missy Pancoast, Sue Edwards, Talia Moser, and Turia Pope. To those of you in the all-girl band, Touché, don't give my drum job away while I'm out signing autographs!

And lastly, thank you to Mom and Dad, a.k.a. Virginia and Bayard Van Hecke. ("Mr. Van Hecke" came into my life when I was eight and ever since he's been my one and only dad.) You repeatedly offered to help in any way you could, but I figured after four decades of dealing with a wandering daughter, be it when I was three years old and marched myself across the Mississippi College campus; when I told you I was in the southern hemisphere, but changed my mind and ventured way up the latitudinal lines far into the northern hemisphere; when I would call home to say I'd made it to a destination only to get back in the car and keep driving; or when I obligingly made collect calls from exotic locals around the globe, but refused to wear a dog-collar ID in case my body washed up on shore, you've done all you need to do and you deserve a break, at least this once!

Foreword

By Curtis Wilkie

For anyone with a long memory, the thought of icehouses creates the same nostalgia as recollections of service stations with real service, drug stores with soda fountains, Sunday nights with Jack Benny on the radio, and six-ounce bottles of Coke that sold for a nickel.

That era may have passed, but Elli Morris brings it back to life in "Cooling the South," her affectionate look at the business that once sustained her family in Jackson, Mississippi, and helped the South endure sweltering summers in the days before air conditioning and refrigerators.

The book reminds me a bit of "Beautiful Swimmers," William W. Warner's wonderful appreciation of the struggling, old-fashioned watermen who toiled for their living in the Chesapeake Bay.

Like the dying craft of these fishermen, there is something magical about icehouses and iceboxes, chipped ice that cooled drinks and colorful snow cones in paper wraps that disintegrated into delicious, nice messes.

Romantics recognized a primitive power about the man who delivered the product. Eugene O'Neill used him as a metaphor in his play, "The Iceman Cometh." A sports figure who performed well under pressure was known as an "iceman." Hollywood used ice picks for exotic murder weapons and heavy tongs as symbols of strength.

In the French Quarter of New Orleans, the streets sang—only a few decades ago—with the cadenced clop of mule-drawn wagons bringing blocks of ice to bars and restaurants. There are still elderly patrons of Galatoire's who maintain that the elegant establishment started to go downhill when their cocktails were no longer filled with ice chipped off the block.

Elli Morris has the same sort of sentiment about a time in America that has receded too quickly into the forgotten past.

"History books have let the manufactured ice business down," she writes. She is right, for there is little record of the ice trade beyond tattered copies of old trade journals. Elli Morris pored through many back issues of *Refrigeration* and other magazines as she gathered information for her book. "I discovered," she says, "a huge hole in American history. I discovered a larger story than my family history, larger than even the state where we had our business. I discovered an entire region profoundly affected by the manufacture of block ice and how valuable that industry was for our nation as a whole."

Photo by Ryan Norton.

Before we had the electric Frigidaires that kept perishables from spoiling and managed to freeze ice in trays, we depended upon the icehouses. I was a child in the 1940s, and I remember. As surely as we looked to coal deliveries to keep our furnaces going in the winter, we anticipated the regular arrival of blocks of ice to store in wooden chests in order to preserve food during the warm months.

At one time, in the twentieth century, Elli Morris writes, the ice business was so vital to our national interests that an iceman could be excused from war duty.

She introduces the ice business at the very start of her story, telling us that she lived in her family's shut-down plant for a year when she was thirty-eight years old. "I suppose I shouldn't tell you that, it sounds like I'm a vagrant or a hermit but if you're one of the lucky ones who have ever been in an old block ice plant, with the looming machinery, the various sections of multi-leveled floors, stairs and elevators, then you might understand my craziness."

Elli Morris is neither vagrant nor hermit nor crazy. She's an artist and a poet and a photographer, and she displays all these talents as she takes us on a search for her own lost ice age. Along the way, we learn that the expression, "a chip off the old block," came from a father-and-son ice operation; that the mob in New Orleans once "iced" an enemy by tracing him to Canton, Mississippi, preserving his body in a 300-pound chunk in the local icehouse; that an enterprising ice company that sold eggs and milk on the side became the precursor of today's convenience store. I was also pleased to find that the big icehouse of my childhood, a formidable red brick building in McComb, Mississippi, situated along the main line of the Illinois Central Railroad, still stands. It's now a fashionable nightclub, called, appropriately, "The Ice House."

Time passes, as quickly as ice melts. The icehouses gave way to higher technology, to central air conditioning, state-of-the-art refrigerators, and neat little ten-pound bags of crushed ice that can be bought for a buck at most any gas station. Yet the mystique of the icehouse continues to exist for those of us old enough to remember, and for those who have Elli Morris' book to evoke a special time.

CHEMISTRY

Ties That Bind

Water is weird—thanks to the hydrogen bond

Just because water is everywhere—percolating through the ground, hovering in clouds, sloshing around our cells—doesn't make it any less weird.

Water dissolves a lot of the basic rules of chemistry. Most substances get denser as they turn from liquid to solid form, their molecules stacking up neatly like boards in a woodpile. But water doesn't do that. If it did, the ice cube in your drink would sink. Water expands when it freezes, forming latticelike structures with lots of gaps between molecules. Instead of a woodpile, ice molecules are more like a house.

Squeeze most solid substances in a vise, and they become denser and they break into pieces). Squeeze ice in a vise and it gets denser by turning to a liquid. Release the pressure, and the water turns back into ice. The principle works with glaciers: The weight of the glacier creates a liquid layer at the bottom that helps the glacier to slide.

Another anomaly: Water has a higher boiling point than many other substances. It's a good thing too. If water had a lower boiling point, the oceans would long ago have evaporated into the atmosphere, and Earth would be a lot more like Venus.

Scientists think they know the main reason for water's peculiarity: the hydrogen bond. Admittedly this concept is not the most evocative in the annals of science, but perhaps it's all in the inflection. Try saying suavely, "Bond. Hydrogen Bond."

A water molecule will typically link up with four others via this bond—each of the two hydrogen atoms in water grabbing an electron pair in different, nearby water molecules. These bonds have just the right amount of stickiness. It's a Goldilocks situation. You wouldn't want the bonds to be too weak, because water molecules would break apart and would be essentially useless. And if they were too strong, says chemist Martin Chaplin, "you wouldn't get much flow, and water would behave more like glass."

Chaplin studies the way the hydrogen bonds in water affect biology. Think about what life is: ordinary matter in a highly organized state. Where does the organization come from? Chaplin suspects the hydrogen bonds in water. Liquid water may seem loosey-goosey—the way it feels, splashes around, drips, puddles, forms a bead. But in biochemical terms, these qualities are signs of structure.

Water is the lubricant, the grease that makes biochemistry possible. Water has given us oceans, clouds, rivers, lakes—and it helps shape everything alive on Earth. So the next time you stand on a beach and admire the beauty and vastness of the sea, or marvel at a seashell, remind yourself: It's all brought to you by the hydrogen bond.

—*Joel Achenbach*
WASHINGTON POST STAFF WRITER

Boiling Hot? Maybe Not.

Water boils at 100°C—or 212°F—scalding hot by human standards. But that's at sea level. The boiling point of water, or any liquid for that matter, is determined not only by temperature but also by pressure. At higher altitudes, say in Denver, where atmospheric pressure is lower, the boiling point of water is lower too. Cooler boiling water takes longer to cook pasta (ten minutes in Cincinnati yields linguine al dente; after ten minutes in Denver your noodles are still crunchy), but it's also cooler to drink. People at very high altitudes (in Tibet, for example) can drink boiling hot tea without burning themselves. In the near vacuum of space, water at any temperature boils away because there isn't enough pressure to keep it liquid. —*Heidi Schultz*

▸ **WEBSITE EXCLUSIVE** For more about water and for links to Joel Achenbach's work, go to Resources at nationalgeographic.com/magazine/0405.

HEAR

America's rural interior searches for new horizons

After years of drought and depopulation, many parts of the Great Plains again meet the 19th-century definition of frontier territory: an area with no more than six people per square mile. As farmers and ranchers forsake the heartland, native prairie, native buffalo, and Native Americans are staging a comeback.

A THUNDERSTORM HALTS HAYING IN NEBRASKA'S SAND HILLS
ARTHUR COUNTY, NEBRASKA

THE FAMILY BUSINESS

I used to live in an ice plant. I suppose I shouldn't tell you that, it sounds like I'm a vagrant or a hermit but if you're one of the lucky ones who have ever been in an old block ice plant, with the looming machinery, various sections of multi-leveled floors, stairs and elevators, then you might understand my craziness.

I lived in the shut-down ice plant for one year when I was thirty-eight, up in the old-fashioned 1930s style office where there was little in the way of heat or air. This particular plant happened to be my family's ice business, the Morris Ice Company, a business we'd had for over one hundred years. The building I inhabited was our second location, on a one-way street right by the railroad tracks in downtown Jackson, Mississippi. In general, the neighborhood was so deserted everyone drove the wrong way on either side of the one-way section, but the tracks in the center lane still brought forth a tiny bit of commerce—usually at 2 a.m. when I was trying to sleep. I cannot give you any worthwhile reason why I lived there, except for the pure intrigue of it—and for the fact that I'd always wanted to live in a big abandoned warehouse. Although the ice business had ceased twelve years before my arrival, the property never sat idle. Some of the rooms became storage depots for junk from various family members and the large tank room was currently housing a taxicab repair shop. Hebron Morris, my uncle, the past president and current daily supervisor for the property, never let the place look abandoned, keeping up the rose garden out front, giving seasonal color to each flower box in the fifteen-foot-tall windows and the sections of ground right below.

I'd always been intrigued with the old ice plant, photographing the machinery each time I came home for a visit but I never dreamed it would one day become my home. Auspiciously, when I returned to Jackson in 2000 seeking refuge and a place to stay,

the one hundred-year-old family home, a Greek Classic Southern Revival resplendent with paintings the size of grown men, was undergoing a major overhaul. It is a wonderful place to visit, where the maids and yardmen keep it cleaned, polished, ironed, clipped and filled with aromas of the Deep South, but I had little interest in being set up in crisp, white, cotton sheets.

The extensive renovation on the house was the break I needed. My uncle had no choice but to offer me a spot at the ice plant. If he said yes to my plea for a factory life, at least I would be back at home, not out on the road in some foreign country, sleeping under cover of fallen leaves until I got a ride to the next cool spot on the map. Cloaked in that dubious gypsy reputation, Hebron bequeathed me the floor space of the upstairs office night after night—as long as I assured him I would keep both niece and plant safe.

It was a crazy request, to stay in a place that had very little heat, very little air conditioning, no shower, no stove, no bathtub, no bed, just my quarter inch thick air mattress pad, a cozy mummy sleeping bag, my pillow and a six foot stuffed tarpon hanging on the wall keeping me company. Each morning, I hid my "bed" so Uncle Hebron could come in and keep the daily routine he'd had for the past twelve years. Once he arrived, normally having to awaken this sleeping beauty, he fixed breakfast for us using a small microwave and toaster. He would pull cooking accoutrements out of the cabinets and the tiny dorm refrigerator like a magician pulling out rabbits. He fed me well, both with sliced grapefruits, hard-boiled eggs, slightly burnt

Side door and flowerbed of MICO; MICO, circa 1927.

Photo by Ryan Norton.

toast and more importantly, with stories of the long-gone ice days. We had our breakfast in the old office where only the photographs on the desks have changed since the 1930s, each of us occupying one of the large wooden desks scattered across the hardwood pine floors, our breaths frosting in the cold room as we conversed of plans and pasts.

After breakfast, Hebron would go on about his day, suited up in tie, jacket, coat, and without fail, a gentleman's dress hat upon his head—except when he wore a straw hat for gardening. I'd head in my flannel pajama bottoms and pea coat to the same country club where many years before the staff had taught me, as a three-year-old child, how to sign my initials so the bookkeeper would know whom to charge for the French fries and pickles. The current staff only scolded me once for going through the lobby still wearing my slippers—a clever ploy designed to distract attention from my PJs. I'd shower there, then head back to the factory to work on my ultra modern orange laptop while Hebron pecked away on his typewriter, using carbon copies for reports on the myriad of business ventures the company still dabbled in. Oscar and Felix of Odd Couple television fame would have been right at home.

Each evening, I became the official gatekeeper of the family's frozen treasures, a virtual museum in waiting for this curious photographer/nosy journalist who took her turn at the ice plant by sifting through the old papers and old memories like a welcoming pack rat. Little by little, I was falling in love with the unfolding history of a lost industry.

My first nightly challenge lay in securing the plant, a building that was never designed to be sealed off from the inside. Each front door of the ice plant was graced with a sturdy outside padlock, making it impossible to lock myself in if I entered from that direction. If friends dropped me off, I could get them to fasten the padlock on the outside so Hebron could open it come morning. Otherwise, I had to lock the front doors, then traverse around to the back of the plant and walk in the pitch blackness across the factory floor, dodging strewn metal car parts from the taxi cab repair shop. If I bumped into something, I'd immediately hear the scurry of wild cats jumping away or a bird squawking at me as she retreated to a distant rafter.

Hebron Morris, President, MICO, 1967-1988.

What always hit me upon entering, though, was the familiar smell of the factory, rich with oil, dirt and the stench of leftover ammonia. Just one whiff triggered vivid memories of the plant as it had been at full operation, loud, busy, dangerous and lit with sunlight streaming in the fifteen-foot tall windows put in for cross ventilation. Others have a dog awaiting them at home; I had stoic engines and lingering odors of activity. Navigating to the other side of the two hundred-foot by one hundred-foot vast expanse of darkness with my shins intact and my toes unstubbed always brought an immediate sense of accomplishment. Pain-free or not, I moved on until I slowly bumped up the first set of stairs that opened into the greeting area, ever-so-slightly illuminated by the street lamps out front which gave me just enough light to get the key into the first interior locked door. Behind this door awaited a second set of stairs, a tiny landing, sharp turn to the left and more stairs up

THE FAMILY BUSINESS

to the next locked door. There was a light switch for this second set of stairs but if I turned on the overhead light, I'd just have to come right back down the stairs and turn it off again once I opened the door into the main office. Often (sorry Hebron) I left this second interior door unlocked for my own easy return, assuming no one would break in. Such were my nightly activities simply to enter my humble abode. The only times I ever left, once entrenched, were to pilfer fresh vegetables from my uncle's garden to add as garnish for delivery pizzas. Regardless of the oddities, the factory was all mine during the nighttime. Come morning time, Hebron regained control of the space to perform regular business activities.

scared me to death, but it was all worth the fright to sneak into the magical ice room, the land of pure enchantment, a fort of incomparable magnitude.

Crinkling, crunching, shattering ice is what I still remember most from the storage room. As an adult, the beauty of the glacially-blue blocks of ice stuns me, but as a child, the sound of walking on white frost and broken chips of ice was beyond cool. Everything else in the rest of my Mississippi world, the mud, grass and pine straw, was a soft, muffled quiet under my feet no matter how hard I stomped. But in the ice room I became a giant from another world, from the moon or Mars or an undiscovered galaxy, a ferocious monster capable of huffs and puffs

When I was a child, the plant was a hub of activity, astonishment and danger. Cars were pulling up, loading and leaving. Big yellow trucks roared their diesel barks at the platform, waiting for their cargo. Gigantic, muscular men were everywhere, made that much larger by the massive parkas they wore against the cold, even when the outside temperature was a thick, dripping, humid bath of 95 degrees. Inside the plant, the smell of grease, iron, ammonia and sweat permeated the air, summer and winter. We had twin natural gas engines, each standing fifteen-feet-tall, that seemed like living breathing dragons. Their two-stroke pistons pounded out energy relentlessly, night and day, just as they had back in the 1920s, 30s, 40s and 50s, resting only one or two days of the year during their annual overhaul. Electricity seemed almost tangible as the generators, attached to huge fly wheels casting off a mesmerizing hot breeze, produced enough energy to light up an electric switchboard rife with gauges, buttons and levers in the front, and a frenzy of tangled wires very much alive with electrical power in the back. I was a hyperactive, skinny "string-bean-pole" child, at home in the top of a swaying pine tree during an approaching storm or bouncing on antique beds until they broke (and I got spanked). The ice factory, with precautions at every turn, and heaving ho. Contrary to my mighty feet, my squeals and screams were stopped in mid-air by the thickly insulated walls and dense blocks of ice. This altered transformation was fantastic. It was freezing. It was short-lived when my uncle shooed me out of the workers' way and pulled me back into the normal life of trees, sun and sky. Hebron was generous with me and the gaggle of cousins underfoot, imparting his father's, and his father's father's passion for a business that impacted their region of America as deeply and creatively as it impacted four generations of the Morris family.

Joseph Morris, the first Morris in the business, never got to experience the awe of ice as a small child. However, as a teenage Civil War Army Captain survivor venturing into the uncharted territory of manufactured ice during the suffering days of Reconstruction, I have no doubt his imagination and fascination soared with each new block of ice produced by his own machinery under his own roof for his own local community.

It was, as my grandfather wrote for a newspaper article on the ice business, "a time when most businessmen would have despaired of opening any kind of enterprise, much less one so farfetched as the bringing of ice for home and commercial consumption into the town."

Original MICO plant on the banks of the Pearl River, circa 1920; Joseph Henry Morris, President, MICO, 1875-1927; Employees of MICO, circa 1900.

One thing is certain. My great grandfather turned the muddy brown waters of the Pearl River not only into 300-pound blocks of ice, he turned that water into gold. In 1880, after five years of working for the railroad industry hauling imported natural ice from depot to depot, Joseph Morris was open for business to create frozen water in the heat of a Mississippi day. Helping him accomplish this monumental task were a brand new, steam-powered ice plant sitting on the banks of the Pearl River where he piped up enough water to make six tons of ice a day; one employee to watch the shop while he peddled his frozen wares up and down the unpaved roads of Jackson; his bright red ice buggy; one mule; a customer base of about 5,000 people; and an enormous determination to make ice.

Surely, the need to support a bevy of family women who, depending on their age, had been left widowed, childless or orphaned by the Civil War propelled him to be a survivor and a hustler. His foray in the natural ice business taught him the value wealthy people placed on ice, but this new, manufactured commodity was cheap enough for regular people to purchase ice for the very first time—if he could convince them of its uses. Touching ice would've been a pleasure but trusting one's daily bread to the stuff must have sounded a bit too surreal to anyone who had seen the rampant devastation a hot day could wreak upon a pot of home-cooked field peas properly seasoned with a good coating of pork fatback.

Yet here this thirty-six-year-old man stood, trying to tell them a hog could be slaughtered at any time, no need to wait for the first frost. Vegetables could be picked and kept fresh instead of pickled and canned for preservation. Milk could be bought from the dairyman and kept cool without lowering it into a well. Even without an "icebox," the first refrigeration device, a poor family could still purchase and keep ice by digging a hole in the back yard, lining it with sawdust and popping a one hundred-pound block down into it.

The inexpensive price of Joseph Morris' artificial ice was on his side, swaying the leery into at least a trial run. As Rose Budd Stevens wrote in her fabulously Southern cookbook, "From Rose Budd's Kitchen," filled with her memories of a time when people were still killing rabbits, possum and deer for their own food and cutting down trees for fuel, "the grandest treat of all was on Sunday, with the family meal, when Mother would sliver off a piece of the ice for us kids to lick like a popsicle." It didn't take long for those living in air as thick and spicy as a bowl of gumbo to figure out a cold bit of ice was a direct piece of Heaven.

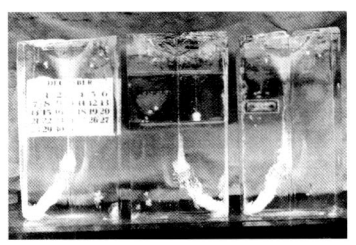

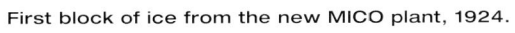
First block of ice from the new MICO plant, 1924.

By 1900, Joseph Morris had a fleet of employees working day and night to supply the increasing demands for ice in Jackson. Already, the business had been profitable enough to pay for the reconstruction of the old homestead, a smaller yet still very palatial version built on the same property where Sherman had left his signature of soot twenty-five years earlier. From the ashes of despair, within one generation, the ice business was bringing comfort and health to everyone in its wake.

Well, almost everyone. Those in the capital city were eager to buy the "man-made" ice, but when country visitors came to town, it was sometimes too new a commodity for their liking. Take the country preacher who traveled to town one hot summer day in 1906. He was told about humans creating ice, something heretofore exclusively within the realm of God alone. He visited the Morris Ice Company (MICO), where he saw with his own eyes ice being made in Mississippi—*in July*. Flabbergasted, he shared this news with his congregation upon his return home. It was all just a bit too much for the good people of his faith—too magical, too demented or perhaps a lapse of sanity. Either the preacher had lost his mind or he had been taken in by the Devil himself, but whatever the cause, the congregation knew they no longer wanted him as their leader and kindly asked him to step down from his post for making such an outlandish claim that ice could be made in Mississippi in the summertime!

One thing always confused me about the original Morris Ice business. Lacking the infrastructure of our modern cities, the original plants were built along rivers and streams for easy access to pump the water needed to produce their ice. In the 1880s, the water in the Deep South had few, if any, contaminates streaming into it like there are today in the twenty-first century. The air, as well, was free of industrial pollutants that plagued the northern, urbanized regions. I understood harvesting ice from remote northern lakes and streams, where the water flows clear over a bed of hard, clean granite, but in the Deep South, we are a land of red clay and rich black mud. The first plant in Mississippi was built in the port city of Natchez on the banks of the Mississippi River, "the Big Muddy." MICO was built on the banks of the inappropriately named Pearl River, not quite as muddy as "the Mighty Mississippi," but darn close, too close for me ever to understand how they made crystal clear ice from either of these water sources.

Then I learned about the settling tanks, where the dirt was filtered out of the water before it was sent to the

Remains of original MICO plant after fire, 1923; Surviving mound of ice after fire, MICO, 1923.

ice-making room. Using distilled water, created from steam engines, was another way early plants cleared the water of dirt and debris. My uncle's face was the best part of this discovery, he as confounded by my view of brown-colored ice as I was of how customers purchased such a thing. Fortunately, my great grandfather never doubted the quality of his manufactured ice, easily convincing natural ice customers to purchase his artificial ice to preserve perishable goods, like milk or butter, or to make their traditional, refreshing "Mint Julep"—a sprig of mint, a shot of whiskey and a good deal of finely crushed ice.

My grandfather, Joseph Henry Morris II, had no trouble grabbling with the notion of artificial ice. He had a brain custom-fitted for the ice business. He loved to tear apart machines and he loved good, honest people. Granddad worked for his father in the ice business before and after college and World War I, seeing the business grow by leaps and bounds during those first decades of the 20th century.

In 1920, he and his father ran an ad in the trade organ, *Refrigeration*, announcing their brand new Frick "flooded system" complete with a set of piping, headers, agitators, accumulators, connections, even a new crane with air hoist, and can dumping. It was full swing ahead in their most modern of ice factories—for three years. MICO, along with its neighbor, the Enochs Lumber Supply Company, had grown into the two most prominent plants in town with bright futures ahead of them. But, one night, on November 6, 1923, both plants went out in a blaze of glory. The lumberyard caught on fire, the wind spread the fire to the ice plant and both were totally destroyed. The yard lost millwork designed for the new, million-dollar Edwards Hotel (a decades-long Jackson eyesore and pigeon nesting factory that is slated to have a second life as chic condos). The ice plant lost everything—except the ice. It held its own, rendered one massive, solid block standing thirty feet high, the scorched roof of the factory still sitting atop the mound. The townspeople set their minds to methods of saving the ice and suggestions poured in to the company. A few betting types had money on how long the mound would last, which was quite awhile in the weak winter sun. Months passed before the last bit finally melted into the river.

I believe the fire was the undoing of my great grandfather, who soon thereafter relinquished control of the business to his vibrant young son. Granddad was eager for the challenge to build the second phase of MICO, to make the business a part of a new era, the world of long distance transportation. When the first plant was built, mule and buggy were the main means of transportation. Fifty years later, railroads had hit the big time for local, regional and long distance transportation of goods and people. Taking full advantage of the propitious moment in time when the fire occurred, Granddad chose not to rebuild on the banks of the Pearl River but to build his new plant in the heart of the commerce district, right on the railroad tracks. The brand new plant, when it opened on December 1, 1924, was capable of producing one hundred tons of ice a day, using twin engines, twin generators and twin compressors. Originally, the motors were electric but they had a tendency to go out during the fiendish southern thunderstorms. When natural gas, a cheap source of power, was discovered in the 1930s right across the river in the next county, Granddad purchased two Bruce McBeth 200 HP natural gas engines, making his operation the first and only ice plant east of the Mississippi River to use natural gas. The only regret my grandfather had with his design, even forty years later, was the crane system, capable of lifting only a modest four cans of ice at a time versus other plants that could pull thirteen.

While he was upgrading to the natural gas engines, Granddad added a new building for crushed ice and built an office on the second floor—the same office that would become, seventy years later, my twenty-first century bedroom. A classic 1930s office with cashier windows cut inside the counters, low

 hanging fluorescent lights, plaster walls and a steady stream of cold air piped out of the storage room, MICO was definitely the coolest office in town.

To contact the office by phone, customers simply asked the operator for "817"—the complete and official new phone number (The old number at the downtown office had been 117, as seen on our old ice picks). As the demand for telephones increased, the phone company added one digit at a time, upgrading the number to 2817, then 2-0817, and finally 352-0817. Otherwise, MICO was a very self-sufficient operation, furnishing its own power from the generators and had its own artesian water from wells. It also supplied these valuable services to the row of duplex houses behind the plant for the measly fee of $24 a month. These types of independent services became a thing of the past as the City of Jackson slowly forced everyone to be dependent on city utilities, but the services came without much improvement. One of the duplex residents told my grandfather, "Their electricity ain't no better than yours was."

In a testimony to his business acumen and sales skills, Granddad propelled the company forward during the Great Depression. While many ice plants managed to stay afloat during those hard times only because the public was completely dependent on ice for food storage, MICO flourished, never experiencing even a setback. In 1933 during the heart of the Depression, Granddad purchased a beautiful thirty-six-foot motorboat, naming it *Lula Dean I*, in honor of his only daughter and second child. Aunt Dean never went on to become an employee of the ice plant, but she nevertheless supported the family business with her numerous social functions and gala events at the Big House, the stately family home.

During his reign, Granddad transitioned from mules to motor vehicles, from small motorized wagons to delivery trucks with eight wheels, from railroad car loads of ice to eighteen-wheelers roaring down four-lane highways. Regardless of the mode of transportation, the demand for ice was great for most of his lifetime. In 1955, a Rotary Club article quoted Granddad as saying, "They keep talking about the demise of ice. Well, I've been here forty years and I sure haven't seen any evidence of ice going anywhere."

That quote is from a period of good times for the ice business throughout the Deep South and good times for my grandfather. With business booming from home and commercial deliveries all over town, Granddad enjoyed the pleasure of a new employee, his third child, my uncle, Hebron Morris. Although his first born, my father, Joseph Henry Morris, III, or "Daddy Joe" as my sisters called him, didn't take too kindly to working side-by-side with his kinfolk, Granddad nonetheless foresaw a bright future for himself and his family. That dream ended in 1960 when my father, who had fled from what he perceived to be the mundane ice business straight into the ice worlds of North Dakota, Montana and Colorado for the exciting gamble of mineral rights to oilfields, innocently sped through a railroad crossing at the exact same moment a passing train was plowing down the tracks, killing him eight months before he and I ever had the chance to meet.

Granddad dutifully reported his son's death in *Refrigeration*, the trade journal to which all of his friends subscribed. By chance, I discovered that small obituary during my research at the headquarters of *Refrigeration* as I sat on the floor, rifling through every decade of the magazine from 1906 until 1975. As my father rejected the ice business during his lifetime, I can only conclude that my grandfather felt the industry was so filled with his friends that he wrote to them through *Refrigeration*, needing to let all of them know what was happening in his life. A happier, albeit quirkier, discovery I made is that my grandfather, my uncle and I all have the same size and shape of head. I can, and do, wear their beautiful "7 1/8 long oval" dress hats, sometimes with permission, sometimes before Hebron can detect their absence from the wardrobe that holds the collection of 150 gentleman's hats. I always return them unless Hebron decides they look better on me, which has only happened once. So far. Despite my sleuthing, I have not been able to determine the hat size of my great grandfather, Joseph Henry Morris, the original Morris Iceman.

1930s office, MICO; Joseph Henry Morris, II, President MICO 1927-1967, shown on the cover of *Refrigeration*.

A few years after my father's death, Parkinson's struck my grandfather. He fought hard, demanding that his male nurse take him to the office every day until he was too weary to work, resting only long enough to gather determination to try it again tomorrow. I was very young when he fell ill, and have few memories of him other than a tall, thin man, looking tall even when he sat in the four-poster canopy bed, unable to take any medicine, not even an aspirin. I was sad not to find an obituary of him, the true Iceman, in *Refrigeration*, alongside so many other announcements of the passing of owners, managers, deliverymen and workers on every level that filled the pages of that journal during the turbulent ice years of the 1960s and 1970s.

Upon Granddad's death, Hebron, as the sole surviving Morris Iceman, was *ipso facto* handed the reins as president of MICO. Hebron knew the intricacies of our business and the ice industry as a whole, but monumental changes were underfoot. MICO began shutting down at night, no longer on the twenty-four-hour schedule it had maintained for forty years. During the daytime, the plant was still teeming with hustle and bustle but with the evening hours quiet, one of Hebron's earliest memories of the ice business became simply a relic from the past. When Hebron was a young child, before air conditioning had been invented, the entire Morris family slept out on the upstairs "sleeping porch" each summer in hopes of catching a breeze. Sleeping outdoors, they could hear the low, deep rumble of the factory engines ten blocks away. The engineer my family had at the time believed the mufflers originally made for the engines decreased the workload so he removed them, leaving the whole town to be rocked to sleep with the assurance of plenty of ice when they awoke.

MICO was certainly profitable as far as the local natural gas company was concerned. In an era when most people used natural gas only for heating in the wintertime, there we were with two behemoths of an engine, each running on natural gas, cranking out power for the entire operation of the business—making ice, running electricity to the office, keeping the huge storage room cold—all of which required a lot of natural gas, about $4,000 worth a month. This was our normal bill, even in the summertime, when just about no one else around town was paying for any gas usage. The gas company had a small monthly pamphlet in which Hebron wanted to place an ad for the Delta States Ice Association. He went down to the office of Mississippi Valley Gas to buy a small ad for his announcement. "Mr. Morris," the sales manager said, recognizing the name on one of the biggest checks that came in all summer long, "we'll give you any size ad you want for nothing."

By the 1980s, the nature of the ice business would not have been recognizable by my grandfather, let alone my great grandfather. MICO was one of the few block ice companies still surviving on the production of 300-pound blocks of ice. Newer equipment cost less, used fewer people and more economically met the new and increasing demand for packaged ice. Block ice plants lost their commercial accounts by the week, month in and month out. Our plant had a few niches that kept us going. Nearby chicken processing plants still had a tremendous demand for block ice. The construction of a nuclear power plant in Port Gibson, Mississippi, took a few years during which time MICO supplied daily deliveries of block ice used to make the concrete.

Random agricultural businesses continued to rely on block ice, as did restaurants, county and state fairs, bars and hotels, and the hometown minor league baseball park relied on MICO each season, regardless of its track record.

Over the years, MICO had transformed from its meager beginnings of a two-person team into a thriving business demanding an entire crew of skilled employees to keep the plant making, storing and delivering ice. Mr. Bankston, the chief engineer; Mr. Jobie Harris, the smooth-talking sales manager; Loleta Dove, the crackerjack bookkeeper; Red, an ice puller and the resident drunk who saved his empty Mad Dog 20/20 bottles in a locker in the back of the plant, where they sat as unconcerned then as they were twenty years later under my wandering eye; Sandifer, the deliveryman who conned the unwary with his dry ice smoking trick; and their nameless compadres from the two eras prior to this crew—they all were MICO.

The plant closed November 1, 1988, after 113 years of continuous business in the same family. Hebron waited until November to close because the summer was still profitable, October is still warm in the South, and that's when the ice-hungry State Fair comes to town, always a big consumer of block ice. The day the plant closed, grown men clung to the railing on the stairs, their vision blurred from hot tears streaming down their faces. All their shared laughter, pranks, jiving and camaraderie, their beloved frozen world, had come to an end.

(above) Chief's desk in engine room, MICO; (right) 1934 Bruce McBeth 200HP natural gas engine, MICO.

Today, the Morris Ice Company factory remains a safe haven for Hebron, a place against the world, his own private home away from home. He still cares for every brick of the 30,000 square feet of buildings and every blade of grass on the five acres of property no matter that we are no longer in the ice business. Everyone in the family understands this, as does everyone at his local bank, the local post office and the local country club. The entire community knows him as Hebron Morris, the Iceman, dressed in his suit and dress hat each day of the week, just as he has been for fifty years.

Although Hebron dearly loves the ice industry and is a walking encyclopedia of that era, I often feel he really preferred the extracurricular activities stemming from the business. This belief is due in part to the confessions by former employees when I asked if they were ever recruited for work out in the garden, which was conveniently located in the back of the ice plant where water was once stored in cypress holding tanks needed to purify the water used for making ice. When the company built a newer system, Hebron co-opted the concrete dividers as separate farming areas for a plethora of Southern goodies—one for collards in the fall, one for cantaloupes, squash and cucumbers in summertime, and one for staked plants including okra, field peas, tomatoes and green peppers. By the back fence sits a peach tree Hebron planted for his mother, a great fan of peaches, on her ninety-eighth birthday. At first I found this gesture ludicrous, but my grandmother lived to be 102, *almost* long enough to taste the fruit of her birthday present.

The gardening, the birdhouse condo clean-up for the annual return of the purple martin birds around February 12, the gathering of buckets of pecans from the massive trees planted in the front lawn when the new factory first opened in 1924—these were pleasant, multi-generational past-times in a business that pulsed with energy and deadlines from day one to day 40,000 (or so).

Some of this Morris Ice Company history I knew before I began my efforts as a block ice chronicler. I knew my family had been in the ice business longer than anyone else in town and that it was one of the oldest businesses in continuous operation; I knew my great grandfather had taken his business from making six tons of ice a day to almost twenty times that before he died; I knew about the determination and ingeniousness of the block ice era from ice stories from my uncle. I knew I loved photographing all the machinery and the idiosyncratic nature of an ice building itself.

I also knew the peculiarities of a year of locking myself into the plant

THE FAMILY BUSINESS

MICO, circa 1974; Oakleaf lettuce, backyard of MICO.

via padlocks, wondering how an ambulance would rescue me encased in those padlocked doors when I thought I was dying from consumption of questionable steamed mussels. I knew the pains and joys of trying to rescue a baby bird that fell into the undrained oil pit of an horizontal compressor; pulling heavy, ten-foot doors open and shut in the pitch black, only to walk across the mine field of discarded automobile parts strewn willy-nilly by the resident tenant; of walking up the tank steps to the office steps to the empty desks and chairs of the office that I reclaimed as a "bedroom."

And finally, I knew that some other life in some other town was calling me away. My personal ice age ended when I moved north to satisfy that calling. But while I was away, all that material my uncle had saved and all that information he held in his head kept nagging at me. No disrespect intended but my uncle and his cohorts are not getting any younger. I felt an urgency to gather this jewel of a story I had been privy to experience into a form I could share with others.

If ever I were going to do it, the time was upon me. In April of 2003, I wrote my uncle with plans to document the business in Mississippi and to visit in the heat of August for authentic images of sweltering Southerners beset with the need for anything cool and refreshing. His letter of reply warned me of the dangers of photographing that which no longer existed, or that was in such a state of dishevelment that I might be in physical danger with each step. As a result of our shared lives at the plant, however, he admitted that he knew better than to dissuade me. He backed this up with evidence in the form of three maps for me to use in plotting my course, one map for each state that made up the old Delta States Ice Association. I discarded Arkansas and Louisiana, sticking with Mississippi as my sole source for my forthcoming book. Ha! Little did I know what I had begun.

During that first, month-long trip hunting for old block ice factories in Mississippi, I put 3,000 miles on the rental car just within the borders of the state, finding everything from a complete functioning block ice plant to plots of land where nothing remained save square concrete foundations. Only my uncle's discerning eye knew they had been supports for massive engines from old ice factories. I visited local public libraries, college and university libraries and the state archives, asking anyone over thirty-years-of-age questions about the block ice business. I spent monotonous hours in front of a computer screen surfing the web for any traces of the block ice era. I interviewed family, friends and lots of strangers, all of whom enjoyed remembering and sharing their memories about block ice.

And, along the way, I discovered a huge hole in American history. I discovered a larger story than my family history, larger than even the state where we had our business. I discovered an entire region profoundly affected by manufactured block ice, and how valuable that industry was for our nation as a whole.

COMMUNITY INVOLVEMENT

When I began exploring the "trail of abandoned ice plants," as my uncle named my ice exploration journey, I was searching for any type of evidence from the block ice era. I'd traveled much of Mississippi during my stint as an audio tech for Mississippi Educational Television so I knew the lay of the land, but I had

very little understanding of how and where block ice had been used. My own ice past was infused with the industrial stories Hebron shared over the years so I incorrectly assumed similar tales lay in wait. Block ice, it turns out, isn't simply a generic item from the past. It had been an integral part of every area of the state, but the uses and needs for block ice were largely dependant on the varied local economies.

Hebron, of course, intuitively understood this and had been working up an itinerary since receiving my letter announcing my intent to become an ice chronicler at large. Dividing the state into its three different regions, the coastal area, the central agricultural section and the northern Delta lands, he'd been contacting old acquaintances to see who was still open and who still owned some of the block ice plants. It was my job to photograph whatever relics and artifacts remained and to put several decades of history into perspective.

Not knowing what I might find at any of the ice plants, I tried not to pre-determine what to photograph, instead letting the icehouses dictate what I needed to document. If the scene called for a striking black and white shot, then I'd be ready. If it were filled with glorious color, I was going to shoot color.

I was photographing with a 4x5 camera, an extremely old-fashioned contraption with bellows like an accordion, requiring a tripod and a black cloth thrown over the photograph's head to view the scene. The quality of a 4x5 image is spectacular, and I figured it was what my colleagues from the block ice era would have used to take a photograph of a new ice plant or a newly-installed piece of machinery. In the commercial world of New York City, this type of camera still rules the roost, although they now use digital backs instead of real film. Because the 4x5 camera body has swings, tilts and rises, all technical jargon for adjusting the lens board and ground glass panel, the photographer has the wonderful ability to manipulate and control every aspect of the image.

It can take one hour to get the camera set up exactly right, adjusting the lens up, down, back, forward and side-to-side until everything you want in the frame is where you want it and in focus. The black cloth that goes over the camera shields the screen from every tiny beam of light, much as you wish you could protect the modern LCD digital images that disappear in bright sunlight. The cloth comes in only one style: thick as a winter coat. I'm not going to describe the adjectives flowing from underneath that cloth in those defunct ice factories filled with suffocating Mississippi-in-August summer heat. Suffice it to say, it can be very difficult to keep your cool when sweat is streaming into your eyes and the swarming mosquitoes have a passion for every ounce of your flesh, right down to the skin on your DDT-soaked fingers. Under such circumstances, it was nice to remember I was simply a visitor to the block ice era, that modern life was waiting for me right outside the walls of the plant with ready-made air conditioning in a green four-door rental car.

Photo courtesy Lynn Brown.

When my great grandfather was starting up his ice business, 125 years ago, life for him and his contemporaries was very different—and much more difficult—than our daily lives are today. We like to romanticize the past, believing life was more simple back then, but life was a lot of work without the trappings of our twenty-first century existence. People got around on foot, by canoe or riverboat and the horse and mule were popular transportation choices. Roads were sandy along the coast, filled in with oyster shells in

Horse and wagon used to deliver natural ice harvested from Round Lake in Charlevoix, Michigan.

some places. They were made of bright orange mud in the central part of the state and deep black soil made the paths and roadways in the Delta. I doubt many people had hour-by-hour daily calendars, not giving a hoot what every thirty-minute internal held in store for them. More important were the seasons—the loveliest time of fall, then the wet rainy cold of winter, the super short yet dramatically colorful season of spring followed by the long, intense heat of summer, climaxing in the hurricane season.

They did have gilded mirrors, paneled oak walls, the Pony Express, one hundred years of the Constitution of the United States of America, ships that crossed the Atlantic and Pacific oceans and a crude sewage system. They essentially had no medicine besides chicken soup unless you are one of the unlucky few who consider castor oil to be more good than evil. The family doctor, more like a shaman with a black bag filled with homegrown herbs and wild forest barks, made house calls exclusively so no insurance claims nor mounds of paperwork for the sick. They had no radios, television, airplanes, soda fountains, drink machines, computers, electricity or telephones. Motorcycles, the precursor to automobiles, were still on the drawing board. A few oddballs rode the latest invention, a bicycle, and I bet it was worth exerting great amounts of energy to experience even a waft of coolness.

When summer pummeled the South, the house would be "prepared" for the humid times ahead. Chairs were draped with slipcovers to protect the cushions from the inevitable drenching of sweat. Paintings and mirrors were encased in mesh cloth to protect them from flies laying their eggs. Beds were clad with mosquito nets for protection against diseases. The nets sound and look romantic, but those tiny, flimsy protection devices trap personal body heat and deny any outside air from reaching you, adding to the heat of the already insufferable night. Often, searching for the slightest of breezes, everyone evacuated the inside beds in favor of the outside sleeping porches. Heavy winter rugs were replaced with thin cooler straw mats. With summer lasting longer than winter, many Southern homes were built with a central

hall to promote drafts and the heat-producing kitchens and smell-producing bathrooms were often detached and built out in the yard.

A few homes had deep wells or cisterns where butter, milk and maybe some cheese were stored in closed containers dangling on a rope in the chilled waters below. It was the only method for keeping these precious foods from spoiling. Chickens were de-feathered for bedding, boiled for lunch and dinner that night—every part put to some household need. Hens naturally lay eggs during the warm months of summer and only produce eggs year-round when they are pumped up with steroids, artificial light and climate-controlled boarding houses—none of which existed in the 1870s. Fresh eggs, then, were a summer treat, pickled eggs a winter stable. Hogs had to be slaughtered in the winter coolness when the meat wouldn't spoil, keeping the entire summer's feeding from going to waste. The scrumptious bounty of a great summer garden was either consumed that day or put on the hot fire of a wood-burning stove for canning and pickling, with the hope the family would be able to absent itself from starvation that winter. In spite of their cunning and ingenuity, people died each summer from the oppressive heat even though they were far more acclimated to such burdens than our modern population.

For the wealthy few, summer's oppression could be staved off with a very expensive, exotic imported freight, natural ice. Southerners paid heavily for the northern ice that had been harvested in the winter, stored until spring then shipped on the long journey down the Atlantic coastline or the entire length of the Mississippi River. In the hot, humid lands of the South even a little bit of ice made a difference and the natural ice merchants knew they had a captive market.

Prior to the greenhouse effect, winters in much of the northern half of the country were cold enough to freeze rivers and lakes. In the coldest days of winter, teams of men and horses harvested this natural ice for their own needs and as a precious commodity for people who had never made a snow angel. They cleared away the snow and rough layer of ice on top using scraping boards. Then, they hitched up a team of horses to saws that cut through the ice frozen two feet thick. A well laid-out grid system, complete with open water channels to get cut blocks of ice from the river to the shore, kept the operation running smoothly—until man or beast fell in the frigid waters. One method of retrieving a horse required men to briefly hold the animal's head underwater which forced the horse to take a huge breath of air when released, thereby filling its lungs and becoming buoyant so the men could pull it out of the water. Barring accidents, waiting crews of men shuttled the blocks into icehouse after icehouse for miles up and down the shoreline. This scenario was repeated on every major river in every cold state in the North. Along the Hudson River there were more than 135 major icehouses in the mid-1800s.

One particularly ambitious man from Boston, Massachusetts, Fredrick Tudor, came up with the bright idea to sell ice to far away places. His first goal was Martinique in the Caribbean. He had a few problems with storage and insulation, so his first run ended up with more water than ice, but he was undeterred and smart enough to learn from his mistakes. His next round of ice, now packed tighter in more sawdust and moss, was delivered as ice. Success upon success in foreign ports emboldened him. In 1833, he successfully shipped more than one hundred tons of frozen cargo on a four-month journey covering 16,000 miles, including two crossings of the equator, to Calcutta, India, where the British were crazy for the stuff. Tudor, America's first "Ice King," sent his fleets of ships to many continents and many ports along the Eastern coast of America. The slower the wind blew, the longer he had to feed the ship's crew, so the more he charged, taking full advantage of the scarcity of his product.

When the Civil War hit, Tudor's ice business was booming with sales to the Union troops, but the Lincoln embargo brought shipments of ice to the South to a screeching halt. This, in turn, improved the smuggling transactions from Mexico, where defiantly hot Texans received one of the new inventions for making artificial ice, adapted from Dr. John Gorrie's 1851 ice-making patent. The Texans put the device to work during the war. After it ended, ice ships no longer came south without King Cotton as a return cargo, and Southerners realized they were going to have to make their own ice if they wanted any at all. The Texans shared the device with their French neighbors to the East, who were the first ones to make artificial ice a commercial success. In New Orleans, at The Louisiana Ice Company, located on Delachaise Street next to the Mississippi River, the very first man-made ice business was set up in 1868. Turning out eighteen to nineteen tons a day per machine, the company couldn't produce enough ice to satisfy the demands of the Big Easy—much less give aid to the rest of the sweltering population of the Deep South.

Tudor and other natural icemen didn't take kindly to the idea of artificial ice. Natural ice was a luxury in the South but in the northern cities, six million people bought four million tons of ice in 1878. With so much at stake, they were "greeting any news of an artificial ice disaster with glee," according to old newspaper accounts. Such a disaster was a common mishap throughout the first fifty years of the ice business because ammonia compressors didn't have adequate pressure release valves and the ice plants had the rather volatile combination of being made of wood and creating their power by burning sawdust. Since the quantity of artificial ice paled compared to the quantity of ice made by Mother Nature, the harvested natural ice businessmen were rather smug about their superior status—until they had to face their own natural disasters.

The first few winters of the 1890s were extremely warm, which forced the natural ice trade farther up into Maine, adding to the transportation costs of the ice. Next, the natural ice trade took a hit from the unaccounted for by-product of the Industrial Revolution—pollution and severe sanitation problems. The rivers and lakes had so much pollution that ice judges would declare an area unsafe. The biggest fear was the rivers, and therefore the ice, might contain the bacteria that causes typhoid.

The tides had turned. Manufactured ice was now unstoppably on the rise all across the country while natural ice was on the way out and gone by 1925 after a hundred years of profit. Northern businesses and homes adapted to the artificial business instantly but the Deep South still had to create an infrastructure that would take ice from luxury and novelty to necessity.

Early on, people relied on manufactured ice mostly in the summertime much as we do now when we buy an extra bag for a cookout or a day at the river. To accommodate the need, the earliest ice plant businesses had two seasons, ice in the summer and coal in the winter. Often you will find old ice picks, given away or sold to customers, imprinted with "Ice and Coal" behind the company name. It seems ironic a hundred years later to think about the filth, dust and soot of coal sold side-by-side with crystal clear, edible ice. At the turn of the twentieth century, both of these commodities required home deliveries, which kept the clientele dependent on the same company throughout the year. Even so, early ice plants were found only in towns with enough population to offer assurance of year-round income.

Electricity, less common than coal for heating for the general population at the turn of the century, was created at ice plants for their own needs from the steam- or diesel-powered engines. Throughout the South, the ice plants would sell their leftover electric energy to an otherwise powerless city. In a twist of events, the Pascagoula Ice & Freezer Company, of Pascagoula, Mississippi, began its life in 1903 as a power supply business, Electric Light & Power Plant, making block ice on the side.

When the Pascagoula Ice and Freezer plant was built, block ice was still pretty much a novelty to most of the coastal community, but as the seafood industry grew, so grew the block business. For generations, men had been living off the fabulously rich fishing in the warm waters of the Gulf of Mexico. Either the families ate the daily catch or they set it over a fire and smoked it dry to hold it over for rainy, stormy days. With the advent of block ice, fishermen could buy a load, put it in the hull of the ship, fish day and night, staying on the trail of a run that would fill up their icy-cold hull. Returning to shore when the run ran dry, waiting customers could buy the catch and use more block ice in their own home refrigerators to store the seafood for days at a time, no longer dependent on having to consume the catch that evening before it spoiled.

Many ice plants up and down the coast supplied the seafood industry but in Pascagoula, the shrimp business took off early and solidly with Mr. Hermes Gautier at the helm. He bought the old Electric Light and Power plant in 1936, when the Great Depression forced the company to sell all five of their plants on the Mississippi Gulf Coast. Mr. Gautier really wanted only two plants, but he had a strong gut feeling about the shrimp business and its potential to bring prosperity to all of Jackson County. He accepted the offer for the Long Beach, Biloxi, Bay St. Louis, Picayune and Pascagoula plants, where he used block ice to pursue his real dream: the inception of "flash-freezing" shrimp to send it across the country and into foreign waters. It was a perfect union of ice and seafood.

Boats would line up along the dock of the Singing River at the edge of Pascagoula to have block ice "blown" into their ship hulls. Blocks were placed into a chipper, a sawing device that diminished a block into fist-sized crumbs within a matter of minutes, three minutes to be precise. A long, six-inch diameter hose and motorized fan were connected to the other end. A dockworker would aim the hose into the belly of the ship, filling up the hull for a one- or two-week trip. If the deck of the boat was hot when the catch was brought on board, it required more ice to chill the seafood, shortening the boat's stay out at sea. Back on shore, the catch was kept cold with block ice as it lay in wait for purchase, set on a bed of crushed ice at the local market. If the shrimp was shipped fresh, as far away as the Rocky Mountains, more block ice was used. Finally, the seafood was stored in the family icebox that used still more block ice. With such demand for ice, the third-generation Gautier business and many other block plants along the Gulf Coast remained healthy far longer than inland ice plants.

A different seafaring industry established in 1938, the Ingalls Shipyard, was a good customer for the long-term operation of the Pascagoula ice plant. Thousands of outdoor construction workers were constantly parched and

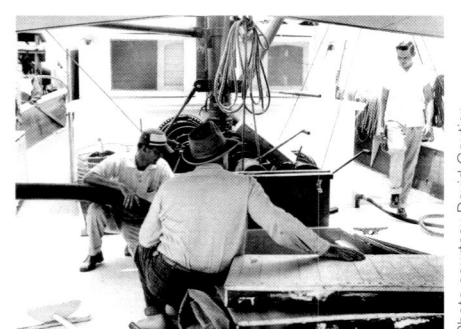

Pascagoula Ice and Freezer Company, circa 1908; Ford-powered ice crusher blower machine, Pascagoula Ice and Freezer Company's dock on the Singing River, Miss., circa 1950; Loading ship hull with crushed ice, circa 1950.

thirsty for ice-cold water in the heat of the summer, guzzling the stuff like it was going out of style. Until the end of 1999 when electric coolers replaced water and ice, the Gautier family business supplied ice for all the shipyard's water coolers scattered over one hundred acres. About twenty tons of block ice per week in the winter and up to seventy-five tons per week in the summer added up to a steady supply of ice all year 'round.

The climate along the Gulf Coast lent itself to the use of block ice in more ways than one. For millenniums, water, wind and sand have intermingled into one determined destructive force during the infamous hurricane seasons, probably creating the Gulf of Mexico and the Florida Peninsula bite by bite. In every hurricane that's hit the area since 1868, block ice plants have been there to help in the recovery. Usually, since the ice plant created its own power from generators, it could be the first business up and running immediately after the storm had passed, operating days before the city could repair public electric lines. The plant would open its doors to a line of people eager to preserve what they had in their home iceboxes, in electric refrigerators and in deep freezes. Since block ice lasts much longer than modern chipped ice, there was a good chance people could preserve their food if they could fend off the temptation to open the appliance door and check if it were still cold in there, the answer changing with each second the door stayed open.

Ice was a necessity for many businesses in the event of a hurricane: hospitals, emergency workers, restaurants and hotels all needed ice. The demand for ice was often at a peak for morgues, keeping bodies from decaying until funerals could proceed. One worker at the Pascagoula plant was asked to take a truckload of ice to the county morgue. The mere image of a room full of the dead was too much for the driver. He got right out of the truck and headed for home, quitting on the spot.

The hurricanes of the 1950s and 1960s—Betsy in New Orleans, Louisiana, in 1954; Fredric in Mobile, Alabama, in 1962; Camille taking down Biloxi, Mississippi, in 1969—demanded tractor-trailer after tractor-trailer loads of ice. Neighboring ice factories always chipped in to help out the affected towns with the unwritten rule that the first load was donated to the community and the following loads sold at regular prices. Icemen never used price gouging on the frantic crowd lined up outside the ice plant, around the corner, down the street and into the next block. The order and the imposed rations of ice per customer were maintained by the National Guard, so urgent was the need for ice.

Residents standing in line for ice following Hurricane Fredric.

Ice distribution was overseen by the hometown iceman. Quin Gautier, son of the original owner of Pascagoula Ice and Freezer, unfortunately had great practice at serving the hurricane victims. He exhibited such wonderful kindness during his reign at the ice plant that his fellow icemen bestowed upon him their greatest award, the McMannis Humanitarian Award in 1965. Later, his peers put their faith in him again by electing Mr. Gautier president of the National Ice Association for 1967. He let none of it go to his head. Instead, he had a great down-to-earth understanding of the situation, specifically that there are two things people need in times of a natural disaster. First, Mr. Gautier said, they need toilet paper and secondly, they need ice. He said he couldn't do anything about the first, but he was always there to help them with block ice.

Amazingly, the ice plant itself has received little damage since its cornerstone was put in a hundred years ago, losing only its roof during one of the big blows. The plant's greatest threat most recently came from the oncoming progress of a ten-lane connector bridge. It would have taken down the dinosaur of the old building had it not been on the National Register of Historic Places. The preservation was lucky for my photographic journey and lucky for the local Boy Scout troops who get to go to their favorite site for a tour each year. It was not so lucky for the three Gautier brothers now running the plant, Warren, André and David. Not only are they trying to make a living in that convoluted archaic space, but they have kept all the old engines, generators and ammonia-cooled freezer room operating as homage to their father and grandfather, contemporaries of my uncle and grandfather.

As ice helped encourage the seafood industry along the coast, block ice enabled the central section of the state to become an agricultural center for fresh produce shipped north and west along the up-and-coming railroad infrastructure. Two brothers, Hugh and William McColgan, opened up a plant in 1904 in McComb, Mississippi, a town that had the typical shortages of the time: very little electricity, no paved roads and a small population with homogeneous skills. The brothers knew how to transform the area by importing a diverse population from other parts of the United States, even attracting people from Central Europe. They put the men to work and created the largest, fastest train-icing operation in the country, thanks to the ice plant's prime location in the crossroads of the strawberry, tomato and bean produce markets of Mississippi and Louisiana. An added bonus was the re-icing of bananas, not a native crop, but they offered substantial ice demand on their way up from the loading docks of Gulfport, Mississippi and New Orleans, Louisiana. The original ice plant, McComb Ice House and Creamery, produced seven tons of ice per day. The plant became the largest in the South in 1924, producing 200 tons a day. In 1926, Xavier Kramer purchased the plant and it became the largest railroad-icing complex in the world. The icing galleries, using electronic conveyors, could load sixty rail cars simultaneously and ice the entire trainload of cars in less than an hour, less than half the usual time. Over the years, the ice plant suffered a set of fires, the first one in 1950 forcing the plant to close its doors permanently. The second fire turned the sprawling complex into a dilapidated eye sore until a creative, ambitious fellow named Dan Jones opened up The Ice House, what he likes to call "Southwest Mississippi's Premier Nightspot." Having much respect for the building's past, the club owner kept the storage room as he found it, without a roof, full of trees and atmospheric layers of moss, evidence of the room's inherent coolness even though the ammonia coils and insulating cork boards have long since gone.

The McComb ice plant, still standing and being used for a new purpose, helped allay my big-city skepticism about finding a barrage of old ice plant locations transformed into un-nameable chain stores, turning America into a land for the lost who never need to know where they are, regardless of their environmental locations. Monotonous landscapes do not make interesting photographs, but I soon learned that most old ice plants, located along the railroad lines, were simply abandoned as worthless property when highways became the primary means of transportation. Encouraged, I delved deeper into the rural areas of the state and headed farther north and west towards the Mississippi River. This rather financially depressed area turned out to be rich in lingering ice plants, not torn down by hungry developers in need of more concrete strip malls.

Up in the Delta, there are no cool springs to jump into to escape the heat. The creeks, already a scary color of tan by mid-June, cannot begin to take the edge off a ripe watermelon. If you try to dig a well deep enough to reach something cool, you'll probably spring a leak into the Mississippi River. Sounds like a pretty good spot to start an ice factory, doesn't it? It was, but the economic impact of ice went far beyond the simple desires for individual luxury.

Ever since the black willow and water tulip trees were cut down to make way for farming operations, thousands of laborers with cotton-mouth throats have longed for something better than a glass of tepid water as a relief against the sun-up to sun-down work. Springtime brought hoeing, row after row, and later in the summer they had to lug long bags and pick cotton with painful, prickled hands. Smack in the middle of the Delta cotton fields is Scott's Ice Company, in Anguilla, Mississippi, population 907. Scott's Ice Company, a rather miniature ice plant, wasn't erected until the 1930s but, all the way up

Fire at McComb Ice House, 1950.

Courtesy of the Enterprise-Journal 1950©. All rights reserved. Reprinted with permission.

COMMUNITY INVOLVEMENT

Yesterday's Patio, The Ice House.

Remains of pump for the artesian well at the Ice House of Oxford; Platform with scoring machine, Scott's Ice Company.

into the late 1940s, it was extremely popular, serving mostly farmers whose laborers gathered 100-150 pounds of cotton per adult per day. The ice business was a solid investment for years in similar farming communities in other southern states whose base depended on agonizing, physical labor.

A modern invention then came along to eliminate the need for platoons of laborers who'd placed such a high demand for ice among southern farmers. Surprisingly, it wasn't big modern machinery that took away the laborers, but rather the extensive use of modern herbicides that kill weeds and in turn kill the need for dehydrated cotton choppers. As the cotton industry transitioned, block ice plants also transitioned and gave life to a very modern industry: farm-raised catfish.

As a child, I remember adults tilting their heads and raising their eyebrows, making funny wrinkles on their foreheads, whenever anyone mentioned this new farming endeavor in the desperate Delta. Catfish are bottom feeders, choosing murky, unfiltered and suspiciously dirty-looking streambeds for their livelihood. How were those crazy Delta folks going to get anyone outside the state to want to buy the fish? How were they going to keep the live fish from turning into baked fish in the newly constructed, small, shallow rectangular ponds sitting out in the middle of that shadeless land? Those hot ponds turned out to be a haven for the sturdy catfish and the business was a lifesaver for Scott's Ice Company. When it was time for the catfish to go to processing plants, the biggest one located in neighboring Alabama, they were shipped live in transportation trucks using block ice to cool the waters and release much-needed oxygen. Scott's Ice Company made only ten tons of ice a day but they kept as many tractor-trailers supplied with ice as came their way. They sold ice-cold watermelon on the side, a delicious novelty in town before grocery stores had cold, sliced melon in the produce section. Blues music and artificial ice—those are the two coolest things in the Delta.

Each plant I found still intact had its roots in the basic needs of the South. It supplied a cheaper product to the masses in need of refrigeration properties, but it also had some special niche that carried it into the second half of the twentieth century. In the northeastern area of the state, in Oxford, Mississippi, I found only the last bricks and mortar of a very famous icehouse with a famous long-lasting iceman, James Barr. Mr. Barr has been in an AP newspaper story reprinted across America; he has been immortalized in paintings, photographs and a poster. He is a real testament to the respect icemen had in their communities. He was "The Iceman" for generations of college students getting ice for their Friday night parties on fraternity row at the University of Mississippi. Then on Saturday morning, he was "The Iceman" for the heavily-padded football jocks during the lingering hot months of the fall semester, who enjoyed the pampered coolness of fans blowing a stiff breeze over six tons of block ice sitting on the sidelines of every home game.

Mr. Barr, who could not read or write when he delivered his first round of ice, ran the Ice House of Oxford under five different owners over a period of fifty-five years. He started as a deliveryman, back from the gates of Hell at D-day. He'd made it through France into Germany and finally back to Oxford, where he refused to travel any further away from home than a three-day return trip on foot. Mr. Barr put nine children through school, none of whom wanted even an afternoon shift at the ice plant after seeing firsthand through their dad's eyes how much work it was. Mr. Barr is a grandfather to eighty children and "too many to count" when it comes to great-grandchildren—about forty-four was the count from a great-grandchild who was uncertain on the dates of a few pregnancies—but every one of them learned from the patriarch that ice was a lot of work.

Ice and beer are always a good combination, but Mr. Barr had a distinctive role at the Oxford plant. For the uninitiated, Oxford had a bad go of it with drunken World War II soldiers who filled the pretty little town square with fistfights, lewdness and passed-out bodies. When it got to be too much for the townspeople, they decided to stop serving alcohol and to send those lost men on to some other unwitting community. The university wasn't leaving, however, and the college-age kids weren't going to stop drinking. They drove to the three county lines nearby, bought beer and stronger liquids, brought them back to town and commenced to party down. This arrangement made for too many already inebriated drivers racing late at night to the county line to get more beer. In 1972, the town made a compromise: to sell hot beer within the Oxford town limits. Hot beer is not good beer, but a large bathtub handily holds a 300-pound block of ice, water and several cases of quickly-becoming-cold beer.

Mr. Billy Ross Brown, one of the last owners of The Ice House of Oxford, had dreamed of owning the plant since he was a child making daily visits from his dad's business across the street to get some blessed ice each summer. He was thrilled to fulfill that life-long dream, but he knew he'd be totally lost without Mr. Barr who was still in the driver's seat at age sixty-five. When someone asked to buy the plant from him, Brown tried to compromise between his desire to own the plant and his fear that Mr. Barr was close to retirement by putting a large price on the building. Brown didn't really expect it to sell, but it did! The last owner, Mr. Charlie Watson, owner of Gardner-Watson Inc. in Tupelo, Mississippi, kept it running for a few more years, as Mr. Barr was not quite ready to retire. In the early 2000s, the plant was sold for land development, leveled and replaced with condominiums. If you had a child or were a child that went to Oxford, you knew Mr. Barr and you (as the child) loved Mr. Barr! Oxford now serves cold beer in its restaurants, but hot beer is still the only beer sold in convenience and grocery stores, so this iceman, in particular, is missed when the urge for a cheap, cold beer hits.

Camaraderie seems to be the memory most icemen have of their days in the business. It is with little wonder, as the need for ice seemed insatiable. From 1868 through the 1950s, the number of ice plants grew exponentially throughout the South, such were the good times for the ice business. Only during the 1960s and 1970s, those last couple of decades when the well was drying up, did icemen have to scramble to get whatever business they could, temporarily altering the disposition of a community whose prosperity had brought out their best. For several generations, the old icemen had shared knowledge with each other, helping out when one of them took on a contract too large for his own plant to handle, and selling their extra machinery to a fellow iceman in need. Taking that posture of generosity and concern to their local, state and federal governmental levels of politics, icemen served as state congressmen, mayors, even United States senators. These lasting icemen showered me with knowledge and opened up their businesses and homes to me, my invasive camera, my notepad, tape recorder, my boyfriend/assistant and his video equipment. They told me story after story, explained the inner workings of mammoth machines left sitting in dangerously dilapidated buildings and trusted me to show their business in a good light that would not get them in trouble with OSHA, the U.S. Occupational Safety and Heath Administration. They enabled me to make my dream come true, in part because it was their dream, to write the story of their family ice business that was quickly disappearing from view.

COMMUNITY INVOLVEMENT

Billy Ross Brown, former owner of the Ice House of Oxford.

COMMUNITY INVOLVEMENT

Courtesy of Robert Jordon 1989©. All rights reserved. Reprinted with permission.

James Barr, former manager of the Ice House of Oxford.

THE GORRIE FACTS

After five weeks of photographing and interviewing icemen in Mississippi, my time and money had come to an end. However, I already had a new goal in mind: to visit the "Holy Grail of Block Icedom." Every iceman I met during my research inquired of me, "Have you been to Apalachicola, Florida, to see the Gorrie Museum?"

"No, I haven't," I replied, over and over again until, so embarrassed in the presence of my heroes, I knew before the next round of interviewing took place, I was going to have to visit the state museum regardless of how far it was from Richmond, Virginia, where I was living at the time.

I got the break I was hoping for within six months. I had to return to Mississippi to edit the segment of a television show I was producing on block ice for the statewide PBS program, *Mississippi Roads*. Rekindling my determination to be an efficient researcher, my boyfriend and I headed out for Mississippi two days early by way of a 350-mile detour east and south to the coastal town of Apalachicola, in the panhandle of Florida.

Those two extra days of traveling changed my life. Literally! I changed where I lived. I changed my job. I changed my photography studio. I changed my friends, but I kept the same boyfriend. All it took was one drive-by along Highway 98 on the "Forgotten Coast" and we began plotting ways to move there. The beauty of the area quickly made us realize we were fed up with being so poor in the cold climate of Virginia and the easier lifestyle of the tropical sun beckoned these two carefree outdoor enthusiasts.

Apalachicola, Florida, is a beautiful quaint little Southern town, a bit too quaint for my liking, but the undeveloped natural areas east and west of town resonated with my soul. Unhindered views of the crystal clear waters of the Gulf of Mexico follow alongside Highway 98, a two-lane highway relatively free of traffic. Rather than a constant stream of billboards and shopping malls like you find in other areas of Florida, palm trees, pines and wildflowers are the only things you see between the highway and the sugar white beaches. Looking inland, one finds thick dense woods and dark foreboding swamps replete with lurking alligators and biting turtles.

The area has long been a beacon for agricultural commerce and weary travelers as well as being historically significant as the hometown where Florida's Constitution was authored in 1838. The Apalachicola River, with a 20,000-square-mile watershed dumping into the Apalachicola Bay, gave rise to the town becoming a huge cotton distribution center in the early 1800s and a prosperous salt mining trade, a vital commodity used for the preservation of foods. After the coming of the railroads took over river traffic and the Civil War ended the cotton trade, the stately baldcypress trees growing throughout the area swamps became the economical backbone, harvested for lumber and drilled for pitch, a product used as heating oil and for lanterns. And as glowing balls for a fiery game of Hot Potato by young restless boys growing up in that area during the Great Depression. Today, the area is in the throws of a real estate bonanza, where investors hope to—and succeed in—quadrupling their money within a year's time. A clash is brewing between distant investors, caring only about their own financial profit, and those who have a vested interest in the quality of life the slow pace of the area has provided long-time locals, Canadian Snowbirds in the winter and South Georgia tourists in the hot summer months of beach, sun and tan.

Locals, tourists and the irresponsible share the area with one other type of resident—bugs. June brings biting Yellow Flies. July is vicious Deer Fly Month and August is showered with the meanest, most aggressive Black Flies I've ever lost blood to. All the while you are defending yourself against those daunting attackers, there are the summer-long no-see-ums and sand fleas. But one must never forget, nor underestimate, the perpetual mosquitoes that have been harboring in the swamps and marsh grasses of the area far back in time, at least to the 1840s when Apalachicola was one of the three largest ports in the Gulf. The seafaring people of that time, who knew and certainly detested these insects as much as we do today, did not understand how these insects wreaked so much havoc on their community nor did they know that the havoc would be the source for much relief.

Malaria and yellow fever were rampant in Apalachicola in the 1840s. The causes of the deadly diseases were unknown and, although there was quinine for malaria, neither preventive vaccine nor cure existed for yellow fever. Mysterious waves of death spread throughout the area. The summer of 1841 brought a particularly deadly wave, wiping out sixty-nine percent of the population up and down the entire Big Bend area of Florida.

The terror was so great that entire areas would be quarantined and yellow flags flown. Fever, accompanied by shivering, was the first sign of the disease. In a day or so, the victim would become jaundiced. One or two days later, either the fever had broken and the patient was on the mend—or dead. People tried anything to stay well: Gauze was hung over beds to filter the air; handkerchiefs were soaked in vinegar; garlic was worn in shoes; bed linens were soaked in camphor—the place must've stunk to high heaven!

Desperate to curb the numbers of deaths, the locals debated about filling in the smelly marsh grasses along the water's edge, hoping to kill two birds with one stone. Fortunately, this scheme never materialized, leaving intact the breeding grounds for the abundant aquatic life that supports the seafood in the bay, one of the richest natural estuaries in the country. About the only certainty with yellow fever was that sailors who stayed aboard ships at night in highly infected districts were far less subject to the fevers than those who went ashore during the nighttime. This was good news for the transients, but of no help to the locals being so viciously attacked.

One doctor, Dr. John Gorrie, born on the island of Nevis in the Caribbean, spending his childhood in Charleston, South Carolina, but educated in the colder climates of New York and New Jersey, noted the fevers took a natural holiday with the coming of the winter seasons. Dr. Gorrie also noted that such fevers did not exist in the north where he had received his medical schooling. Perhaps, Dr. Gorrie thought, the disease would disappear if he could chill the air.

Inside his home, Dr. Gorrie had two hospital rooms equipped for observation and treatment of fever patients. In one of these rooms, he suspended from the ceiling an urn containing chunks of natural ice. Next, he cut a small hole in the roof to connect a pipe to a compressor located on the roof. The compressor forced air through the pipe and over the bucket of ice.

Portrait of Dr. John Gorrie, by Charles Foster, 1935.

An outlet pipe, placed low down to the floor inside the patient's room, allowed air to escape. Dr. Gorrie believed the coolness would give the patient some comfort from the fever, and he hoped it might even kill the disease. This procedure was a great act of compassion and medical determination on the part of Dr. Gorrie.

Natural ice was an extravagant commodity when Dr. Gorrie rigged up his cooling apparatus. Natural ice, harvested from the lakes in northern climates of New York, Michigan, and Maine, arrived via sailing ships packed in moss for insulation. If the ships showed up on time, the ice cost five cents per pound. If the winds didn't cooperate, ice became an even more precious commodity, the price rising upward of fifty cents, and sometimes even $1 or $1.50 per pound. In northern climates where transportation costs were minimal, natural ice sold for thirty-three cents per *one hundred* pounds.

In Florida, in the summertime when the fevers were at their peak, the temperature at the top of a ceiling in a room without any air conditioning would be eighty-five degrees by 9 a.m., soaring rapidly to well over one hundred degrees by mid-day. Adding to the heat was the thick, oppressive humidity, often reaching one hundred percent—and it wasn't even raining. No matter what price Dr. Gorrie paid, a pound of ice would not have lasted three hours!

One hot summer evening in 1845, as the story goes, either his maid or his nurse failed to shut down the steam engine on the compressor, leaving it running all night long. The next morning, when Dr. Gorrie made his rounds of very convenient in-house calls on his patients, he realized the air was no longer flowing from the machine. He climbed on the roof and there, in the middle of the Florida summer heat, he found ice on the coils of his machine, made from the nighttime dew condensing and freezing on the pipes.

Already receiving much town ridicule for "trying to freeze his patients to death" with his air compressing machine, Dr. Gorrie really got an earful when he confided with his best friend, a botanist in town, Dr. Chapman, saying "I have made ice." "The Hell you have!" Chapman replied.

Confident, Dr. Gorrie began creating a new ice machine, applying the firsthand knowledge he'd gained by accident: air, when compressed, gives out its heat and in expanding, absorbs it, rendering it latent. The expanding air would absorb heat out of water, producing ice.

Only three years after Florida's statehood, Dr. Gorrie submitted his patent petition to the United States patent office on February 27, 1848, writing "I... have invented a new and useful machine for the artificial production of ice and for general refrigeratory purposes." Dr. Gorrie was granted the first United States Patent, #8080, for mechanical refrigeration on May 6, 1851.

Official record books show a few kindred spirits across the globe applying similar concepts to various inventions for "the water to be congealed," as Dr. Gorrie wrote in his patent application, but Dr. Gorrie's machine was the first truly practical model of a mechanical ice-making machine. The basic principal he used in his machine is the one most often used in refrigeration today, namely cooling caused by rapid expansion of gases involving a change of state.

Dr. Gorrie had hecklers in the Apalachicola area and he was gaining notoriety on a national scale. One New York writer quipped: "There is a crank down in Apalachicola, Florida, a Doctor John Gorrie, who claims he can make ice as good as God Almighty." What Dr. Gorrie actually claimed, according to a footnote in one of his articles, was that "with a machine on a large scale, a ton of ice can be made on any part of the earth for less than two dollars."

The highly profitable natural ice trade kept a jealous eye on the news of Dr. Gorrie's invention. Fredrick Tudor, the Bostonian whose idea to sell ice around the globe earned him the title, "The Ice King," is suspected, but has never been confirmed, of spearheading attempts to sabotage Dr. Gorrie's new enterprise. The unbeatable price must have spurred the underhandedness of the giant distributor but even he could not always control the outcome. On one particular occasion, one of Tudor's greatest enemies, the weather, gave Dr. Gorrie the upper hand.

In 1850, summer arrived early in Apalachicola, causing the citizens in the port city to use all the available ice supply long before the arrival of Bastille Day on July 14. Monsieur Rosan, a native of Paris, a highly cultured gentleman and resident Apalachicola cotton buyer, discovered there was no natural ice to be had for his annual celebration and no more ice ships were on the horizon. The British cotton buyers of Apalachicola delighted in his misfortune. Not to be outdone, Rosan, Dr. Gorrie and his good friend Dr. Chapman conspired to form a plan to get the British cotton buyers.

The Monsieur offered a wager that he would not only furnish ice the next day for his party but declared the ice would be made in the dining room of his friend, Dr. Gorrie. With a basket of delicious imported French champagne—the only "sparkling wine" produced back in the 1850s—offered as spoils for the winner, the Brits promptly took the bet. "To the utter astonishment of the guests, whose curiosity was excited to the highest pitch," writes historian Raymond B. Becker, the three men won their bet as they introduced Dr. Gorrie's ice machine to the public for the first time, rolling it into the dining room. At the toast that evening, Dr. Gorrie was exuberant with his success. Little did he know it was to be the greatest moment of his life, from that time forward his endeavors to promote his new invention would be throttled at every turn.

Try as he might, Gorrie was unable to overcome economic, scientific and moral obstacles in his path to develop the ice machine on a commercial scale. He met with resistance everywhere he went, in Cincinnati and New Orleans, even in Europe as he searched for financial backing. Dr. Gorrie's last years were spent in disappointment and sadness from his failures and criticism. Dr. Gorrie never gave up on his dream, just on his fellow man, understanding his invention was "in advance of the wants of the country."

The last sighting of Dr. Gorrie was on his upstairs porch, wrapped in a blanket, malaria the suspect of his withdrawal. No one knows how he died, only that his continued efforts for the artificial ice business came to an end on June 29, 1855.

Shortly after Dr. Gorrie's death, fellow artificial ice scientist Ferdinand P. E. Carré, from France, made the important discovery that rapidly expanding ammonia changes state at a much lower temperature than air, enabling it to absorb more heat, hence making more ice more quickly. In 1860, Carré received his own United States patent for the development of the closed ammonia absorption system still in use today. Just as Dr. Gorrie predicted, the acceptance and desire for artificial ice caught on all across the South and across the world, giving him the recognition which he was unable to achieve in life.

The following list of honors bestowed on Dr. Gorrie posthumously offers a testament of his contribution to society:

THE JOHN GORRIE STATUE, a marble carving given in 1914 to the National Statuary Hall Collection in the United States Capitol building in Washington, D.C. With numerous well-known explorers and politicians from whom to choose, the state of Florida elected Dr. John Gorrie to be one of its two allotted representatives.

THE GORRIE STATE PARK, incorporating Gorrie State Square in Apalachicola, Florida. The land was granted to the state by the City of Apalachicola in 1955.

THE JOHN GORRIE MEDAL, given to University of Florida College of Medicine graduating seniors considered "most likely to be general practitioner."

A DECORATIVE WOODEN CIGAR BOX, giving Dr. Gorrie credit as Inventor of Artificial Ice. Federal tax stamp dated 1910.

THE JOHN GORRIE ELEMENTARY SCHOOL built in Tampa, Florida, in 1890.

THE GORRIE BRIDGE, a 26,000-foot-span connecting the east and west sides of Apalachicola Bay. The bridge, consisting of two causeways, two bridges and a high draw span over the ship channel, was officially named in 1951 but the community began referring to it as the Gorrie Bridge in 1935 when it was first open for travel.

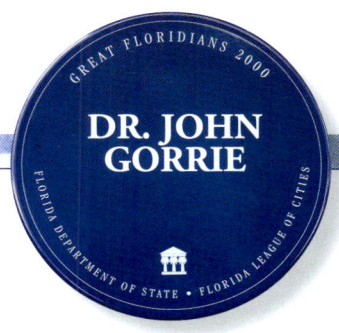

THE JOHN GORRIE JUNIOR HIGH SCHOOL built in Jacksonville, Florida, in 1924.

The distinctive title, "**FATHER OF AIR CONDITIONING AND MECHANICAL REFRIGERATION**."

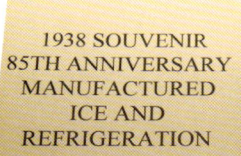 

In 1899, the Southern Ice Exchange erected **THE GORRIE MONUMENT** in the Apalachicola square, adorned with an urn like the one Dr. Gorrie hung from his home for his yellow fever patients.

THE SS JOHN GORRIE, a naval ship built in 1943. The Liberty Ship navigated the Atlantic, Indian and Pacific oceans on twenty-one voyages during and after WWII, before joining the Nations Defense Reserve Fleet in grain storage in Oregon in 1957.

The preservation of **GORRIE'S FIRST MODEL ICE MACHINE**, housed in the Natural Science Museum of the Smithsonian Institute in Washington, D.C. That first diminutive machine took eight hours to make one eight-inch plate of ice.

ICE AND IRON

During that first trip to Mississippi in August, my uncle Hebron handed me a copy of a 1936 ice trade journal, *Refrigeration*, with a photograph of my grandfather on the cover. Hebron said the magazine, originally called *ICE*, had been around since 1906. Several weeks later, while waiting to interview Charlie Watson

of Gardner-Watson, Inc in the northeastern section of Mississippi, I came across a modern issue of the same magazine. Inside, they had a two-page spread "From Our Archives." I loved it! It had funny ads from the era I was researching. It also had a photograph of four women, clad in 1947 "bikinis" that came up to their waists, sitting at a table made entirely of blocks of ice in which four roses were frozen solid. It was the kick-off campaign for National Ice Cake month, June 16–July 15. This sounded like a good place to get some more information for my project, so I wrote down the phone numbers and the mailing and e-mail addresses for the parent company, Yopp Publishing.

Back home, I got Jean Herrington, editor at *Refrigeration*, on the phone. She graciously told me they had all the issues back to 1906 but had no way of looking up any subject matter. If I could give her a date, she could pull out that issue, but to check on information on "the history of block ice," was impossible. "You could come down and look through the magazines yourself," Ms. Herrington said. With no means to finance another ice journey, her great idea was shelved as an impossible idea by the end of the phone call. I would have to content myself with the Internet. The vast virtual world of information turned out to be practically devoid of block ice history, so I started another savings account, determined to one day make it to the treasure-trove of information waiting at the ice journal archives. The savings account wasn't doing too well, but the earlier trip to the Gorrie Ice Museum and to my home state ended up being cheaper than I'd allotted, particularly because I now had a used, really economical car rather than having to rely on the rental arrangement again. I had money leftover and I knew just where to spend it.

I double-checked the address of Yopp Publishing. The magazine had moved from its longtime headquarters in Atlanta, Georgia, to its new home in Beaufort, South Carolina. Beaufort is only about thirty miles from Hilton Head Island, site of one of my many past homes and a place where I still had friends with available floor space for a few nights' stay. A couple of weeks later, I was on my way to the beach and to the headquarters of the oldest ice journal in the country. Once in town, I Xeroxed, I took notes, I set up a makeshift photography copy stand. I sat on the floor for one week riffling through seventy years of history, learning an amazing amount about the rise, dominance and decline of the 300-pound block ice business. Inside those pages of history, I found reference to one man, "Mr. Block Ice," they said, who knows more about the industry than anyone else. Five months later, when I was soliciting financial backing for the project with my homemade pamphlets, I put Mr. Block Ice, a.k.a. Mr. Walter G. Ribeiro, Sr., on one of the twenty envelopes and dropped them all in the mail. Walter wrote back. And wrote more letters, sent more brochures, emailed and thoroughly filled me in on the past and present status of the block ice business as he knew it.

Walter Ribeiro returned from World War II to his home in Philadelphia, Pennsylvania, where his father, Mr. Albert L. Ribeiro, Sr., and his brother, Mr. Albert Ribeiro, Jr., were running the family business, Ice Plant Equipment Company. Walter began calling on ice plants along the eastern seaboard and the central states as a sales representative for IPECO, building his reputation year-by-year as an authority on block ice plants. Ribeiro marketed the family's own low-pressure air agitation system for producing clear block ice, among many other items sold by IPECO. During the one hundred-year era of block

(left) Fairbanks Morse armature of a 1940 10x10 Frick ammonia compressor, Pascagoula Ice and Freezer Company.
(above) Walter G. Ribeiro, IPECO.

ice, there were many thriving manufacturers and suppliers of equipment used in conjunction with the block plants.

As time went by, the large block ice equipment manufacturers, such as York Corporation and Frick Company, saw the approaching decline of the block business and made their move into more modern equipment for air conditioners and the refrigeration business. Rather than simply abandon their old customers, these firms made deals with IPECO to continue supplying parts for their old machines. When the "on-premise" ice machines began replacing the block ice machines, most supply businesses went with this industry trend and abandoned the block business. Not Walter. He stuck it out in the block ice world, dedicated to the industry, knowing every nut, bolt, dog can and crane for all the block ice machines.

IPECO gained the rights from other distributors to manufacture the specifics for each of the replacement parts. They purchased other suppliers, or their client base, and the blueprints for all the knobs and nozzles. Walter and IPECO is a major reason the ice plants that lasted were able to survive. It was hard enough for an iceman to get a mechanic to work on the humongous old ice machines, much less not have the parts needed once someone showed up. IPECO is still a major source of supplies for the various types of block ice machinery that exist today.

The IPECO plant is like a hardware store, filled with possibilities for every conceivable job. The schematics of machines, chart specifications for parts, and intriguing tools for the trade are living pieces of history that fortunately are still part of the everyday working world, not just relics in a museum collection. There are engines, generators, compressors, 300-pound or 400-pound ice cans, can fillers and dumpers, brine coolers, high and low air pressure air systems, cranes and a multitude of other equipment, all used to satisfy the hunger for a chunk of glacially blue soldiers of cold.

There isn't a state in the union where icemen don't know the name of Walter Ribeiro. He knows where the plants are, what plants are operating, how many are in each state, who runs them, how long the place has been in business, and if they produce 300-pound or 400-pound blocks. His reputation is true glacial blue. His generosity to anyone needing a helping hand in the ice world is up to the minute, eager and exact. Walter is ninety-one years of age and still goes into the business two days a week, but the next generation of Ribeiros, his son Walter Ribeiro, Jr., is now at the helm of the seventy-three-year-old family business. IPECO is still a vital participant in the ice world, selling parts not only for the old machinery but also for more modern ice-making machinery and supplies. Walter is indeed "Mr. Block Ice," without whose help I would never have gleaned the whole picture of how an ice plant worked, what made them tick and how they cranked out so much ice for so many decades during the heart of the twentieth century.

Making ice is quite complicated. In theory, of course, it's simple: You take water, chill it below thirty-two degrees and you've got ice. Technically, you have to take the heat out of the water, which, for one hundred years, required an amazing amount of know-how, specialized machinery and power. An average plant required a slew of people to keep it in operation. There were engineers to troubleshoot all the machines, ice pullers using the crane in the tank room, men stacking ice for storage and others cutting the blocks into manageable sizes. The office had women collecting cash, sending out bills and running the entire paper show. Salesmen were essential, getting new contracts for the business. Advertising became a big issue as the industry transitioned from having more clients than production capacity into the latter years of trying to hold clients on block ice rather than seeing them switch to electric refrigeration or fragmentary ice.

None of the business ran itself. All the machines had to be hand-tended, from the massive engines to the hand-cranked adding machines the women used in the office. There must have been a sense of satisfaction in using those large, old calculators, having to physically yank on the handle to get an answer to

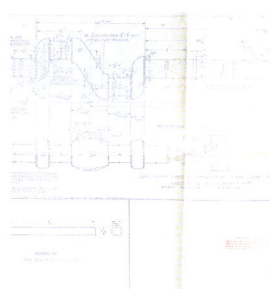 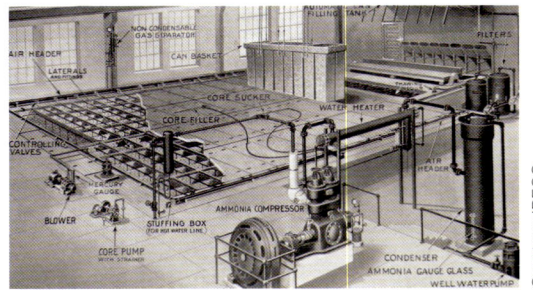 

Circa 1929 blueprint for an 8x8 Enclosed Refrigeration Machine Crank Shaft, Roanoke Valley Ice Company;
Illustration of a typical block ice manufacturing plant using "Air Agitation" system for producing clear ice; Circa 1935 Burroughs adding machine, MICO.

The block ice era was one of craftsmanship and cunning, when machinery was big, tangible, logical and inventive, not to mention beautiful and fluid in its practical design. For those with a penchant for metal, the intrinsic artistic appeal of the machinery is wonderful to behold just for the sake of beauty. In our modern "IT" age of brilliantly fast transference of knowledge, information and communication, compacted into tiny, tinier and micro tiny chips, cells and pods, the inner workings of an old block ice plant can be a fascinating glimpse into the classic era of might and muscle. Look inside a modern freezer and think about transforming it into a space large enough for an entire crew of people to wander around in, work on things, check the ice, move it around, sell it, and start all over again. What now takes up less than a cubic foot of space in the kitchen used to take up several stories and fill up 30,000 square feet of floor space in an old ice factory.

frustrating accounting questions, much like the by-gone days of being able to slam the phone receiver down on an unwanted caller. Certainly, there is no doubt the heavy office machinery sounded better than today's high-pitched, bass-less electronics. This very hands-on approach with large machinery, when labor was the way of the business world, wore one out by the end of the day. Whether you were working in the sweltering heat of the engine room, battling the freezing temperatures of the storage room, walking up and down the stairs to the tank room, or tweaking machines with wrenches that are twice as long as an adult's arm and just about as thick, the job resulted in a full body workout with a strong back and powerful arm muscles for the men and women of ice and iron.

The buildings themselves had to be unique to accommodate the drastic changes in temperatures and functions. The brick walls of the storage rooms were three-feet thick and in the larger ice plants the storage rooms towered several stories over the rest of the building, making an ice plant very easy to spot. Another telltale sign was the loading dock that ran half the length of the building, giving plenty of space to load trucks and for customer pick-up. Fifteen-foot tall windows that opened in individual sections graced the walls of the engine rooms to let out the heat generated by all the machinery. The tank rooms were long expanses of open space, devoid of the usual support beams that would have interfered with the cranes moving up and down the room picking up the blocks of ice. With or without the machinery, the buildings are striking and worthy of preservation.

ENGINES

I don't have an engineering degree—mine is in forestry—so I don't completely understand the technical workings of the old engines. I do find them fascinating to look at, live with and photograph. These old machines have an inherent beauty in their shape, very functional but with graceful lines that helped define the look of integrity. Built of dense iron, they are slow, reliable, simple in construction, and above all, long-lasting. From the small original ice machine Dr. Gorrie wheeled out into his living room, the ice machinery became grand in scale, extremely hands-on in operation and the craftsmanship was unsurpassed.

"State of the art" steam-powered engines ran the very first plants in the late 1800s, using coal or sawdust. The steam engines ran generators that produced electricity for the entire plant—and often for the neighborhood or entire community. An added benefit of keeping coal on hand for a coal-powered engine was the chance to sell coal during the winter when the ice sales fell off sharply. When coal prices quadrupled during World War I, many ice factories switched over to new sources of energy for their power machines; most plants turned to diesel engines or electric motors. Generally, the engines were cranked with compressed air, which got the one or two long pistons moving, in turn getting the attached flywheel rotating. The flywheel got the twelve-inch pistons back to their starting place, and around and around it would go. Given a good overhaul by someone who understands the mechanics of the machines, a fifteen-foot-high single-piston 1928 diesel engine would fire right up by activating the air compressor starting button—albeit with a dense cloud of dust and grime. Some plants relied on their 1920s or 1930s machinery until they shut down in the late 1970s or 1980s.

Once the machines were up and running, they ran at incredibly slow speeds compared to today's machinery. Fairbanks Morse Engine, a modern manufacturing company dating back to the 1870s, came out circa 1913 with a new, faster engine with a top speed of 120 rpm and 12 hp, rather than the 2500 rpm on modern small engines. Surprisingly, the torque of the old engines was tremendous, just the opposite of how machinery runs nowadays. My uncle Hebron says of the momentum and the speeds of the old machines, "They're slow but they got a lot of 'mo.'"

Making up in stature where they left off in speed, the engines were so large they were outfitted with a ladder to get to the open loom of the firing mechanisms. Perched on one-foot-thick concrete platforms necessary to support the weight of a machine made of solid iron, the engines were so heavy they could lift a forklift! When Hebron needed an engine moved once, he called someone with a Caterpillar forklift. The man and his machine showed up and they attempted to lift the engine, but instead, it was the Caterpillar that rose up in the air. At wits end, Hebron called the offices at the Caterpillar Company, but no one had any idea how to help him. Instead, the fellow on the other end of the phone told Hebron he was on his way over to the factory to see the event firsthand because he'd never heard of anything lifting a full-sized forklift off the ground!

1915 Fairbanks Morse 120HP diesel engine, Pascagoula Ice and Freezer Company.

New technology was constantly emerging and the dawn of the "automatic plant" was predicted in a 1930 *Refrigeration* article. "The days of hand control and regulation of the various operations and functions…are numbered. The ice plant of the future will approximate more closely the automatic control than ever before." This version of automatic control meant the thermostat had been invented! Every piece of machinery required manual operation by skilled labor personnel monitoring the functions by sight and sound all day and night. There were no computer chips to tell the workers when to oil and no LCD schematic telling the worker what was wrong when a machine broke down. The plants could not be run without an engineer on duty every hour of operation. Some ice plants even set up small apartments out back of the plant so the engineer could be available any hour of the night in the event of an emergency.

The Morris Ice Company had two matching Bruce McBeth natural gas engines installed in the plant in 1934 to take advantage of the discovery of cheap natural gas in the next county. They ran 24/7 until the late 1950s when business no longer demanded that rigorous schedule, but the machines kept running, on demand, until we closed in 1988. Baby boomers think they penned the "24/7" concept, but those old ice-making machines continuously cranked out ice for an insatiable audience, decade in and decade out. Multiply thirty years times fifty-two weeks a year, running seven days a week, for twenty-four hours a day, minus the forty-eight hours they were shut down for overhauling each year, and you come up with 260,640 hours. What of our modern technology can possibly stand up to such rigorous demands? My pretty orange laptop computer is only five years old, and some days I can hardly make it operate!

For those icemen who didn't get into the business early on, but bought into it during the surplus days of military liquidations after World War II, the latest versions of engines were smaller and faster. However, even these "late models" were all but impossible to work on by the 1960s. The men who knew most about these large engines were steam-engine mechanics, left over from that era in the railroad business. No one else had a clue what to do with an engine whose head gasket was large enough to wear like a hula-hoop! Slowly, even these mechanics were no longer available to help out at the ice plant, so today's block ice owners have to be their own mechanics with knowledge of how to take apart the engines and put everything back together in time to get back to making ice and trying to make a profit.

(clockwise) Rocker arms and firing mechanisms for 1934 Bruce McBeth natural gas engine;
Suction and discharge valves for 1924 Vilter horizontal compressor; 1945 7x7 Frick ammonia compressor; 1932 9x9 York ammonia compressor.

(clockwise) Ten-foot tall fly wheels with leather belts, Pascagoula Ice and Freezer; 1924 Synchronous Electric Motors, MICO; Electric lines leading into back of 1934 electric switchboard panel, MICO; Front of 1934 electric switchboard panel with refrigeration gauges, MICO.

GENERATORS

The old engines might be big and tall, but the first thing you notice in the engine room is the gigantic flywheels that are so much fun to photograph. They loom into space, weighing upwards of two tons. Early on, the wheels had leather belts on them because rubber was not an economical commodity until after World War I.

Once the engines were going, they spun the flywheel, which in turn pulled the generators and ammonia compressors at the same time. The generator took the energy of the engine and converted it into the electricity that ran everything else in the plant—small electric motors, the crane in the tank room, the lights in the storage room and office and the agitating motor for the brine. It made the plants very self-sufficient, able to rebound back into operation after any natural disaster faster than most other businesses in town.

The generators sent electricity to a switchboard panel. Those old switchboards would make any modern engineer or representative from OSHA buckle at the knees and start running for the door. When you look at all the wires running everywhere, you expect to find some Hollywood "Mad Scientist" lurking in the background, vials of bubbling concoction surrounding the unrecognized genius. The switchboard at the Morris Ice plant is still active, not used much since we no longer make ice, but it is no place you want to let two feet of curly red hair loose. When I needed to switch the power on or off while in my industrial home, I wrapped my locks tightly before ever setting foot behind the metal curtain. In our long business history, MICO never had one accident from the switchboard. It is safe; it just looks so intimidating compared to the modern concealment of energy. Block plants were not concerned about such things so everywhere in an old plant, there are telltale signs of how much power it took to make ice. All that power, with the engine, generator and compressor all running at the same time, created a lot of heat. The really tall windows helped dissipate the heat and let in more light in the work area. Some plants had windows on both sides of the room for cross ventilation. Heat, windows and light—it all seems incongruous with water turning into ice, but it's exactly what it took to make block ice.

COMPRESSORS AND CONDENSORS

Like the engines, the compressors were slow and steady, tolerant of the changing conditions of an ice plant where humidity and temperature variances are invasive. They came in various sizes, 6x6, 7x7, 9x9, 10x10, all describing the size of the piston cylinder  and its accompanying stroke in inches. By 1930, two cylinder compressors were becoming more common. Some plants used fuses in the electric motor of the compressor. If you are going to get a mammoth engine, generator and compressor working in unison, you cannot use any ordinary fuse. You have to find one that matches the machinery, of course. Those big, old foot-long fuses, dating five generations back in technology, don't carry such higher amperage, they're only 600 amps, but they're housed in such an incredibly big shell that one fuse weighs in at four pounds!

One of the unique compressors was the Vilter horizontal compressor. Vilter began making them in 1882 for Corliss steam engines and by the 1920s they were described as "high speed" compressors with an RPM of 130 to 175! The pistons rest on their side, taking up a lot of room, but they have a push and pull on both sides of the stroke, making them extremely efficient. My grandfather, Joseph Henry Morris, favored these horizontal compressors when he designed the new plant in 1924. They were tortoise-like, but they were persistent, supplying power at each end of the crank and not losing any work time on the down stroke.

Most people consider the compressor to be the heart of a block ice plant. It is an ingenious part of the plant, basically the recycling center, which helped the earliest artificial ice plants reach their desired goal of creating ice for under $2 a ton, something the natural ice trade believed impossible. If ammonia gas were free, there would be no need for a compressor. But, almost nothing is free, so the compressor allows the ammonia to be reused over and over again. It was Ferdinand Carre', of France, in 1859, experimenting on ammonia gas, who discovered its much lower compression temperature and improved on Dr. Gorrie's ice machine that used air as the compressed gas.

Ammonia is naturally in a gaseous state. The compressor increases the pressure on the gas, which in turn elevates the temperature of the ammonia gas. The condenser then reduces the gas into a liquid under pressure. The ammonia liquid travels from the condenser into a holding tank called the receiver. The ammonia is released out of the receiver through an expansion valve into a pipe where it is no longer under pressure and it quickly reverts to its at-ease stance, which is a gas. When that change of state happens, from a liquid to a gas, the temperature of the ammonia drops radically to well below freezing. This really cold gas travels through coils submerged in brine in the tank room, under the water cans and removes the heat from the water so it can turn to ice. The heat once in the water is now in the ammonia gas that travels back to the compressor where, with help from the condenser, it will once again be squashed into a liquid, on and on, never losing any of its strength, power, fortitude or character.

The simplest way to think of a compressor is to think about a bicycle tire. When you pump air into the inner tube, it is forced into a confined shape, being compressed into a circle. When you depress the valve, the air feels cool to the touch as it is released from the compressed state into its expanded freer natural state. Part of the job of the engineer at the ice plant was to use intelligence and care as he brought the compressor on slowly, tightening the bypass valve and slowly opening the expansion valve at just the right time and in just the right order so the ammonia wouldn't leak and he wouldn't ruin the compressor.

Ammonia is an excellent coolant but it's also a noxious deadly gas. No matter how hard the engineers tried to open the valves slowly on the compressor and keep all the pipe fittings snug and tight, every block ice plant had a lingering stench of ammonia. Ice plants had gas masks on hand in case of a massive ammonia leak. If a leak got out of hand, the caustic vapors would burn lungs and air passages, possibly causing death.

The funny thing about ammonia gas is that it can rise or settle, and it's unpredictable. Icemen became oblivious to the fumes, but others in the community were not. My uncle Hebron recalls times when the fire department would come running up to his plant, ready for a disaster, asking "Where's the ammonia leak?!" No one in the plant would've noticed that the emergency pop-off valve on the condenser had opened, but businesses several blocks away reported an ammonia invasion from a cloud that had floated out of the plant and settled down on them. Other times, Hebron says, the leak would be more contained within the property, the ammonia gas cloud choosing to settle in the backyard of the plant where he had his garden, burning his new crop of peas or watermelons, which he did not take kindly to! When you work around something so hazardous, you get rather used to it, evidenced by this corny joke from *Refrigeration* in the February

1924 Vilter horizontal ammonia compressor, MICO; Circa 1950 ammonia gas mask kit from IPECO, MICO.

1920 issue: "What's the difference between ammonia and pneumonia? One comes in drums, the other comes in chests."

The development of "more stable" synthetic refrigerants in the 1920s, in particular Freon, propelled the efforts of the mechanical refrigerator. These new "safer" chemicals removed the need to be concerned about toxic danger and odor from ammonia leaks. This sounds great until you fast forward to the 1970s when Freon became famous for its role in the drastic depletion of the earth's ozone shield.

TANK ROOM

Unlike the engine room where everything was out in the open, large, bold and densely packed, the tank room where the water freezes into ice was devoid of machinery. It looks like an empty room at first glance, planks of wood placed like a puzzle in a long rectangle. The "floor" was actually the removable tops to each set of ice cans. All the ice was tucked under these planks where you could walk as though you were treading over the tops of unmarked old graves, certain you should not be walking right where you were, but not knowing exactly where else to walk. In the South, the wooden tops were often made of cypress. A hundred years later, they make for good-looking outdoor coffee tables for those fortunate enough to be in the know with great long-term family connections. The wood feels right at home out in the sun and rain and salt air of the Florida coastline, originally designed to withstand the abuse of water, salt and constantly changing temperatures found right at the union of engine room and ice.

This deceptive room began to reveal its secrets as soon as a lid was lifted from the false floor. The first sign of the freezing ice nestled below was the steam, created from the contrast to the ambient room temperature, regardless of summer or winter. All you saw was the very top of the block of ice, the "cake" of ice. Depending on how long that particular cake had been sitting in its frigid "oven," you could see eleven inches by twenty-two inches of water, water turning into ice or solid ice. In reality, that cake was almost four feet deep, hence the constant walking up and down stairs when you worked (or lived) in an ice factory. The cans of water sat in a vat of brine solution, which is simply regular old saltwater, that won't freeze until it gets down to -6 degrees. The cold ammonia gas, inside coils in the brine solution, is what made the brine cold. The iceman tinkered with the exact temperature of the brine by adding more or less salt to it, normally keeping it around zero degrees. To make sure only the water in the cans froze, and not the brine, a motorized agitator with a propeller attached to a shaft, or sometimes nothing more than a boat propeller, kept the brine slowly circulating evenly throughout the tanks.

The cans containing the fresh water were made of metal, so the colder temperature of the brine could easily remove the heat of the water until it reached thirty-two degrees, when it turned to ice. The brine, being saltwater, is very corrosive, so cans were made of galvanized metal, but they rusted all the time, causing icemen to be on the constant lookout for good-conditioned, used cans. Sodium dichromate, added to the brine to help protect the cans, was stained green like antifreeze, so if you had a green block of ice, you'd know you had a leaky can and a block of terribly salty ice. The brine, if it had the right mixture of salt, chemicals and water, was as good an investment as the old pieces of machinery. Home Ice Company of Laurel, Mississippi, used the same brine from 1938 until at least 1968!

The most common dimensions of the cans were eleven inches by twenty-two inches by forty-four inches, a throwback to the natural ice harvesting days. Each held thirty-nine gallons of water, which weighs about 325 pounds, just a tad over the official size of a "300-pound block." There were a few southern ice companies, such as the Cristina Ice Plant just outside New Orleans, Louisiana, that originally used 400-pound cans, but mostly this size was used around Chicago for railroad transportation. Eventually, everyone gave them up—they were just too heavy and cumbersome

Under ideal conditions, it took about thirty-six to forty-eight hours to make a 300-pound block of ice. Keeping the brine near its ideal temperature of zero was critical. When the temperature went up even ten degrees, it took a lot longer for the cakes

Looking down into tank containing brine stained with sodium dichromate.

Anderson Peters pulling ice, Pascagoula Ice and Freezer Company.

to freeze solid. On the other hand, if you tried to freeze a cake too fast, it would no longer be as dense, wouldn't last as long, and wouldn't have its signature strength of freezing so hard the ice could cut you. It could take up to twenty-four hours for a block to melt, sitting out in the summertime!

Making the cake solid was only half the battle. When the artificial plants got into business, natural ice customers already had a preference for the look of their ice, preferring river ice to pond ice. In rivers, as fast as ice is formed, the current carries the air away downstream, leaving absolutely crystal-clear ice. In ponds, the air is trapped in between the freezing water, giving it that cloudy look of home freezer ice. How to replicate a moving stream in a stationary ice plant presented the artificial icemen with a major challenge. The very first plants used steam boilers to produce distilled water, which freezes clear. As coal prices rose in the 1910s and 20s, this extra step became too expensive an option. Sometime in the 1910s, the Air Agitation System came to the rescue with a simple way to force air into the cakes to keep the water in motion as it froze.

This system was the most popular choice for smaller operations, but, like everything else at the plant, it was a laborious method for producing the desired results. Getting on his hands and knees, a tank room worker had to insert a "drop tube" into the top of each cake. Making bubbles in the can, low air pressure, about two-and-a-half psi, was fed through the tube for the first twenty-four hours until the core was about ten inches thick. From contact with the cold brine, a block froze from the outside toward the center. Air and minor impurities in the water would be kept in motion by the pump,

collecting in the center of the cake. After getting on his hands and knees to insert the tube, the worker now had to go back, right before the cake froze good and solid, and put a suction pipe in the center, or core, of the cake, which pulled out the impurities at the last minute. Ice then became purer than the water from which it was made. After removing the impure water, the worker wouldn't want to fill up the inside core of ice with bad water. Plants always had settling tanks or barrels to clear the water of any minerals prior to being used. This is the water the worker would pour in at the last minute to fill the block up completely, then put the cover back over so the block would freeze in the center.

Often, though, this drop-tube process left what is called a "feather," or air stream, in the core where tiny air streams or bubbles could be seen trapped during the last moments of the freezing process when the water was no longer under agitation. Up close in the lens of a 4x5 camera, these air droplets are gorgeous abstractions like none other. The authentic icemen tried to minimize the amount of feather in the blocks of ice. They were very proud of their clear ice, saying it was "so clear, you'd bump into it."

There was an alternative method for making clear ice. A high-pressure air system fed air into the bottom of the ice cans from inside the tank, eliminating the need to put the tube in at the top. Because the line was inside the brine, the air being pumped into the line couldn't contain any moisture or that moisture would freeze. The diameter of the line was so small that any frozen moisture would keep air from getting into the ice can. Without the air, the water wouldn't be in motion so what came out of the can was the dreaded cloudy block of ice. This system, which included a dehydrator that removed water from the air, was expensive to install so only large plants that pulled over fifty tons a day invested in it.

A defining factor of an ice plant was the number of cans it could pull at one time. Small plants most commonly pulled two or four cans, sometimes up to thirteen cans at a time, by attaching the crane to a bracket system. Large plants, such as Triangle Ice Company in Savannah, Georgia, pulled twenty or thirty at a time, the huge row of cans fastened to a grid or basket. Some early plants had only a simple wheel with no electric motor to pull one can at a time. A rare number of plants had "stationary cans." Once the cakes were frozen, a worker stopped the flow of ammonia through the pipes, which heated the brine just enough to loosen the block away from the metal can, and only the ice was lifted while the can stayed put.

The crane was the only visible piece of equipment in the long open space of a tank room. Hanging from the ceiling, the electric crane went four directions: up, down and side-to-side. Moving in so many directions, this delicate piece of machinery required someone used to the subtle innuendoes as he pulled tons of ice out of the brine. A good ice puller, the man operating the crane, was like gold for the plant. A bad puller could make the crane jump off the track, causing an engineer to be called in, taking him away from monitoring the engine room—sometimes halting production altogether while the engineer supervised an entire crew of men that literally tried to put the heavy crane back on the tracks. Or, if the puller was not efficient, fewer tons would be removed from the tank, fewer tons put in storage each day, and fewer cakes started for another day's production. My uncle Hebron tells a story of an engineer getting so tired of fixing the crane when Mr. Allen Hines, the regular puller, wasn't working it that the engineer told Hebron, "Listen, don't let anyone else touch that thing. If Allen takes a break, it'll be faster in the long run if no one pulls ice until he returns!"

The ice puller maneuvered the cans of ice down to the end of the tank room where he would carefully lower the cans into a water bath, a fountain of water rushing out over the walls of the tank. Then, you heard pop, pop, pop, as each 300-pound block of ice was released from its cold metal can and bobbled the three or four inches to the top of the tank. It's a process familiar to those of us who don't have an automatic ice cube dispenser in our freezer, having to quickly pass the metal ice tray under the faucet to loosen the individual ice cubes enough to pop them out. The ice puller lifted the whole unit out of the water bath, moved it over to a hinged trough where the rack was slowly, slowly, lowered onto its side until that scary moment when out spilled the contents—300-pound blocks of ice let loose, free-wheeling it down a ramp with a resounding, vibrating rushing thud when each block hit the catch wall, drenching everything in its way with a water-park ride face full of water.

There is one story when a crystal clear block of ice came out of the tilting rack with a surprise inside. A puller in a block plant in Canton, Mississippi, located just north of Jackson, emptied the ice cans one day only to discover the body of a man frozen in one of the blocks. The New Orleans mafia supposedly traced the truant man to Canton, where they got their hardened criminal.

With the ice cans emptied of ice, the puller began where he started, by filling the cans with water to put them into the tank where the ammonia coils would do their trick again. In the end, ice puller Anderson Peters of Pascagoula Ice and Freezer in Pascagoula, Mississippi, compares his job to that of making ice at home, saying, "It's how you do when you get ice out of the refrigerator trays. You put some more water in there and put it back in the freezer." But, he acknowledges, the two methods have enormous weight differences!

THREE HUNDRED POUND CAKES!

During my first visit to the ice plants on the Mississippi Gulf Coast, I was thrilled to discover Pascagoula Ice and Freezer still employed their old, ammonia-cooled ice storage room, the land of great mystery I remembered from my own childhood at Morris Ice Company. Walking into one of these ice storage rooms,

chilled the old-fashioned way with ammonia coils which cause the floors to frost over, the walls to turn white, the ceiling to be heavy with ice crystals hanging on the white, frost-encrusted ammonia coils, you pass through a portal into another world. It is magical, like walking onto a Hollywood Inner Galactic science fiction thriller movie set with the see-through glacial blue 300-pound cakes rather like characters in waiting, all their power somehow manifest in their stillness. I'm certain this has always been true, from the days when artificial ice was first manufactured until now, when the block ice plant is an anomaly.

Armed with childhood excitement, I was ready to go inside the storage room and make my first attempts to record block ice in its natural surroundings. As difficult as it is to use a 4x5 camera in the stifling summer heat, I quickly found out it isn't much easier if the temperature is colder—close to one hundred degrees colder, that is. Inside their old-fashioned storage room, where the temperature hovers around twenty to twenty-five degrees, I had to force the screws on the ends of my tripod into the crunchy layer of ice on the floor to create a steady surface for the camera. I couldn't breath when I put my head under the black cloth or my breath would fog the ground glass panel. I slipped on the icy floor each time I repositioned my feet. "Snow" from the low ceiling fell on my head and in my face because my body temperature was melting the flakes off the ammonia coils. I quickly regretted not changing out of summer shorts into winter pants as I watched my bare legs turn from tan to pink then to purple and fill up with goose bumps. Block ice, clear enough that it looks like it isn't there, is also a highly reflective surface. Trying to express the depth of the frozen water requires carefully placed flashes but batteries won't work if they get too cold. To keep them warm enough to function,

I kept them tucked into my shorts waistband until the last minute when I loaded them in the various flashes I had set up. When I finally had all the vertical and horizontal lines of the camera plane parallel and the lights just right, I had to throw it all into the arms of hope, not knowing if the sheets of film would hold up or if they would get too cold to record the shot. I was moving as fast as the slippery conditions and the difficulty of a 4x5 camera would let me, but I knew it wasn't fast enough because it was a Friday afternoon and the guys were sick of being at work and ready to go home. They sat on the bench on the platform, politely waiting for me to take one, just one single photograph.

Finally tripping the shutter and hoping for the best, I had to take my camera and gear outside, through eighty degrees of change, from freezing to scorching, in two seconds. If I had been documenting the natural ice trade of Maine during January, setting up my gear inside one of their ice storage houses, maybe the inside and the outside temperatures would be closer, but there's very little chance, even in the dead of winter, that one of the Gulf States is going to have daytime temperatures hovering around twenty degrees! All the camera gear and I looked as though we'd been dropped in a bucket of water, sopping wet and fogged over. Even my contact lenses reacted to the summer humidity with a glaze of fog.

Beauty and mystery aside, the storage rooms were an integral part of the ice plant, a function of the process and distribution of the business of making and selling ice. They were an absolute necessity for every ice plant to hold its product until peak demand. Because the blocks take days to create, demand would easily exceed supply without large storage facilities. As early as November, ice plants began amassing cakes of ice in their storage rooms, getting ready for that huge swell in sales during the summer months. Many storage rooms were so large they were equipped with an indoor open-air elevator used for stacking the blocks in layers several stories high. Plants in the South often had multiple storage rooms, but in space-deprived New York City, one substantial plant had a storage room five stories high. The largest storage rooms in the South were generally located along the railroad tracks in the agricultural regions of each state where fresh produce required ice for transportation to regional and national markets. Hazlehurst, a town in Copiah County, Mississippi, in the heart of the vegetable-producing area, had a storage capacity of 32,000 cakes but a population of only 2,000 people!

(above) Men putting tar and cork in new storage room, Pascagoula Ice and Freezer Company, circa 1950. (right) Mr. "Eppy" moving ice into freezer room, Pascagoula Ice and Freezer Company; Willy Starks, former ice customer, Clarksdale, Miss.

The better insulated the storage room, the less energy a plant had to create to make and keep the room well below freezing. The first step was to properly design and build the exterior walls of the storage room. Most all plants had walls three bricks thick, insulated with a layer of air, then a layer of cork insulation after that. Tar sealed the outside of the cork, and cypress boards or a thin layer of concrete would finish off the interior walls. Ammonia coils, attached at the top of the walls, supplied the freezing temperatures necessary to store the ice. One of the greatest fears, and sometimes a reality for the iceman, was an equipment malfunction in the storage room leading to a meltdown—not a rapid one but just enough to melt the blocks together into one gigantic mound of ice, making it impossible to retrieve six months of work.

Next, ice had to be moved quickly and efficiently out of the hot ice-making section of the plants into the cool of the storage room, trying to keep the loss of precious frigid air down to a minimum. Cristina Ice and Cold Storage, in Kenner, Louisiana, has a regular, full-size door for the men to drag the cakes into the freezer. Other places, like M&M Ice and Cold Storage Company in Cairo, Georgia, have shoots where the ice puller loads the block, lets it go through the trap door and whoosh! You better move out of the way when that mass comes crashing into the freezer room, eventually coming to a stop just before the wall at the opposite end. Pascagoula Ice and Freezer uses a little secret passage door just the right size for a cake of ice, four-foot high and two-foot wide, which keeps all the cold air in the cold room. A man stands in the storage room beside the door and clicks his tongs together to signal the ice puller on the other side of the door. The ice puller loads an upright cake on a tiny tilting tray and passes it from tank room into freezer room. The man in the storage room grabs the cake off the tray and slides it across the floor into place by the other cakes.

Icemen had to have mighty strong backs and legs to bend down, grab hold of a block with a pair of tongs, upright the 300-pound cake and slide it into position in the pile, hour after hour, day after day. You can read the truth in their muscular, callused hands with veins bulging out, their strength the kind a rock climber dreams of. The blocks are slippery enough to slide across the storage room floor but they can slide too easily, banging into the other blocks or getting chips on the bottom if the puller picked up speed before he reached the stacking pile. Ice could bang a man up if he dropped a block on his foot, beat him up in the front of his shins and smash a thumb left in the wrong spot. According to the well-experienced James Barr, in Oxford, Mississippi, "There wasn't nothing easy about foolin' with ice. It was a lot of work."

The 300-pound cakes of ice sat protected in the storage room where the icemen could wield them but most regular people neither could handle nor needed such a huge hunk of ice. To make a block more manageable, the dockworker would section it up using saws with extremely large, long and spacious teeth to cut the blocks. Some plants had two-handled saws for two men to push and pull in unison but in most places, one man went at it alone. If he knew what to do with the pick, he wouldn't have to cut the block clean through. According to Pops, of Richmond Cold Storage Ice Plant, in Richmond, Virginia, he could "cut it straight, hit a few spots right there, hit it like that, hit it again," and he would have neatly chopped the cake into whatever size the customer wanted—blocks of one hundred, seventy-five, fifty or twenty-five pounds.

Using the hand saw took a lot of time, so in the summer, the icemen would be under much pressure to get enough ice to the customers who were standing in a line at the factory platform. Lines were no good for either side; the ice plant was losing money and customers were losing their patience. A gentleman from Culpeper, Virginia, G. F. Major, superintendent of Culpeper Light and Ice Company, came to the rescue of his plant by inventing an "ice sawing device of his own get up." In September, 1920, *Refrigeration* published an article written by Mr. Major describing the operation of the device and reporting, "Cutting ice is a pleasure. Hot spells have no terrors for us now." His invention had a saw thirty inches in diameter that turned at 1200 rpm, and a motor that ran at two horsepower. Similar "scoring machines" became standard equipment on the platforms of all ice plants. The most common machines accepted a full-sized block in the front end with internal saws that lightly scored the cake in half lengthwise, mimicking the dockworker who didn't cut the block clean through. Another set of saws then made four more marks running widthwise before the block was spit out the back end. The dockworker took over then, once again using his trusty ice pick to punch through the rest of the ice for the desired size.

Most 300-pound blocks weigh in at 325 or so, giving the iceman ample room to cut above the desired size and weight. Just in case an ornery customer doubted the skill of a worker, factories had scales out on the platforms. An anonymous worker told me stories of one dockworker who would get put out with customers who questioned the precise weight of a block he'd just cut for them. Knowing he was already cutting high, he would put the reputed fifty-pound block on the scale where it would read fifty-five pounds. Absolved, he would chop off the excess five pounds and then hand it to the whining customer! Often you see scales on delivery wagons from the 1800s, but most of these were for the natural ice trade whose blocks were far more random in density than manufactured ice cakes.

To satisfy the huge appetites of commercial accounts, the ice worker often had to work with full-sized 300-pound blocks, especially for the railroads, one of the biggest customers for many ice factories. Plants either used a hoist to raise a full-sized block up to the top of the rail car or placed the big blocks, usually six at a time, on a loading ramp equipped with notches on it to keep the blocks from sliding right back down. Either way, more men were at the top of the rail car where they used the hook at the end of a long-handled pike pole to grab the block and pull it over to the top of a bunker. The worker would slam the pole down on the scored block, breaking it roughly in half, and shove the pieces into the bunker. Each bunker held about three tons of ice and every car, with two bunkers, had to be iced down. It took the crew of men several hours to fill the whole train, depending on its length. Once all the bunkers were full, the baffles at one end of the car would be opened, depending on which direction the train was headed, and the air movement over the block ice would cool the produce. A few plants made opaque ice for the railroad business since no one would see it anyway.

One of my favorite stories from Hebron was about the Strawberry Special, trains that carried the most perishable of all perishables, sweet, fresh strawberries, from Ponchatoula, Louisiana to the awaiting Chicago markets. The berries, so plump and juicy, were inclined to bruise and spoil rapidly, especially back in those days when fruit was picked ripe off the vine—not

Chris Fortner, ice puller at M&M Ice and Cold Storage; David Gautier, breaking scored block of ice, Pascagoula Ice and Freezer Company.

injected with ether to induce artificial ripeness. Icemen worked frantically to quickly fill the bunkers with ice, the only means for assuring the Southern treasures would still be luscious commodities by the time they arrived at the northern market. Strawberry Special trains had such an urgent mission, they were the only trains given the green light, the go ahead in front of all other cargo trains. Only passenger trains were allowed the right-of-way as the trains sped the ripening berries and the melting ice from the French Market in New Orleans up to the Windy City in Illinois. Today, the cargo trains have the right-of-way as passengers sit and wait for the moneymakers to speed on by.

Sometimes commercial customers required several tons of ice but they couldn't use it in the traditional block shape. Factories had "crusher slinger," or "crusher blower," machines that could decimate an entire cake of ice in ten seconds, a ton every minute. The machine had a large supple four-inch hose on one end that sprayed a layer of the crushed ice over produce in a railroad car. The "top-ice" was laid on thick, maybe ten tons for a load of cabbage heading from Alabama to Wisconsin, enough so that the train didn't have to be re-iced. The crushed ice not only kept hearty vegetables, such as carrots, greens and corn, cool but also supplied precious moisture in transit.

Crushed ice was often charged by the minute since ice plants knew exactly how long it took their crushing machine to pulverize a 300-pound cake. Cristina Ice Service in Marrero, Louisiana, chose to put their crusher outside on the platform instead of inside the freezer room. For truckers filling up to keep produce fresh in transit or for locals purchasing their daily supply of crushed ice used to keep seafood cold while on display at the fish market, this was a preferable location because they could see—and count for themselves—the number of blocks going into the crusher, not having to hope the men in the back were being honest with the number of cakes crushed. Ever efficient, the ice factories would gather up the frost created from the crushing machines and sell it as "snow," the equivalent to sawdust when you cut up a piece of wood.

Delicate produce, such as peaches, couldn't handle the heavy weight

Sizing machine, Gardner-Watson, Inc.

of top-icing. Icemen still crushed up ice to chill it but instead of putting the ice on top of the produce, the crushed ice got dumped into a large tank filled with water. Before the fruit was put in rail cars or overland hauling trucks, it got dunked in this water and ice bath, called a hydro-cooler, which retarded the ripening process.

Watermen were another big customer of crushed ice, putting it in the hulls of their boats, ready to chill down the elusive catch of the day. Since they couldn't pull up to the platform at the ice factory the coastal ice plants, such as Pascagoula Ice and Freezer, came to them. Commercial or private boats could make a phone call to the ice plant, order the number of blocks needed and by the time they navigated up to the company's dock on the Singing River an ice truck would be waiting with their order. On the dock sat a crushing machine with a long hose capable of reaching into the hull, supplying all the crushed ice the captain could handle.

In homes, people made their own crushed ice using an ice pick to chip pieces off a block of ice in the icebox. If the chunk that chipped off was still too large, they had to steady it with their fingers and keep picking away, the dangerous weapon aimed millimeters away from their fingers. Not everyone liked this method—it required a lot of skill not to stab one's own thumb. Fed up with holes in their fingernails, clever Americans designed genius and ingenious methods of getting pieces small enough to fit into a glass of sweet ice tea. One method used a metal tray with slates one inch wide heated and put on top of the block where it would melt into the block only an inch deep. With only the bottom layer still attached, they'd safely use the ice pick to chip the cube off and plop it into a glass. The one-inch by one-inch by one-inch piece of ice produced a rather standardized cube of ice. It was the birth of the "ice cube." Of course, as you chipped or whacked away at the bottom layer of the "ice cube" many chunks would go flying away or slip off onto the floor. Another invention, the "ice catcher," solved that problem using a sharp edge to cut the bottom layer at the one-inch mark. The device caught each cube inside its attached small bucket.

Each new invention created a slight improvement on a very laborious process, but the idea—to get a uniform, easy-to-use size of ice for personal consumption—was brilliant and the desire on the part of the American public for the ice cube became insatiable. Block plants quickly responded by offering their own versions of an ice cube. Various complicated machines came on the scene, some using water-heated hot copper wire to cut 1-1/4 inch x 1-1/4 inch x 1-1/4 inch cubes of ice, slicing a 300-pound block into tiny cubes in twenty minutes. Most plants chose not to invest in these expensive devices, instead using a grinding machine, that chipped the block into an assortment of sizes, and then a sizing machine to sort the ice. The sizing reels, similar to ones used in the coal business, used a rotating dumping cage with three different sizes of holes: "snow," about the size of sugar; #2, the size of marbles; and #3, producing a hunk of ice that could fit in most drink glasses. Men were very busy inside the freezer rooms, loading whatever portions of a block they could comfortably handle into the grinding machine, then holding a bag underneath the sizing machine, bagging thousands of pounds of ice per day. Originally, the bagged ice went into thick, wet-resistance paper bags. Later on came the exciting new invention of "see-through bags," what we now call plastic bags. Since the grinding machine didn't make uniform shapes, the cube itself was basically lost in the process of adaptation—except for that good ole ice cube tray still around in a dwindling number of home freezers. Those ice cubes are cloudy, don't last as long, and might not be taste-free and odor-free like block ice but the cube has, for the moment, its own form of resilience.

Charles Bridges, former MICO employee.

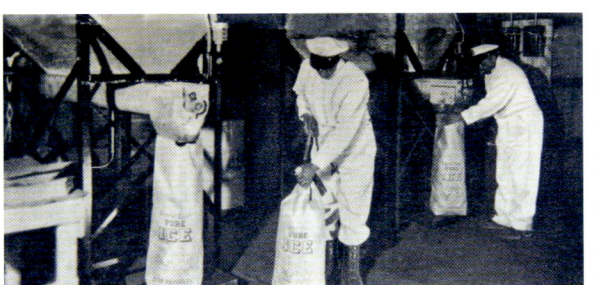

City Products Corporation ad showing men bagging ice.

These "baggonians," as David Gautier and fellow employees nicknamed their job of loading blocks of ice into the grinders inside the ice storage room, had a cold job standing in the freezer room starting at 6 a.m. and not coming out for a break until 10 a.m. or so. I remember as a child how odd it was to be sweating in shorts, playing barefoot around at the ice plant in the warmth of the summer sun, when a man would appear on the platform wearing a huge, bulky parka, its hood covered in what looked like snow, massive boots on his feet and gloves covering up his hands. Customers would drive up, sweating in their cars because most people didn't have air-conditioned automobiles, and melt just a tiny bit more when they saw the man cloaked in such heavy cloth. Their first reaction was to feel sorry for the man and say, "What've they got you doing?!" But in truth, he would be coming outside for a few minutes to warm up, to escape the frigid twenty-degree air. While standing outside to thaw out, he would get as drenched as I did after photographing the ice in the storage room. With his hands wet, his toes wet, and the crystals in his hair melting down his neck, the bagger could only withstand the freezing temperatures for thirty minutes at a time for the rest of the day. Given the choice between working in the ice storage room or putting tar on a roof for eight hours a day in the grueling Southern summer sun, the baggonians, according to Charles Bridges of the Morris Ice Company, had the best summer job anyone could have.

Every ice storage room was wrapped on one side by a very distinctive and memorable feature of an old block ice plant, the platform, or "flatform" as some of the men called it. When I was driving around looking for ice plants in small Southern towns or in the industrial warehouse district of bigger cities, the platform would always catch my eye, especially if the plant didn't have a tall storage room. Immediately, I'd know I'd found an old ice plant.

Most platforms were about ten feet wide and almost always covered to block the sun. The length varied according to how much room each plant had but the height was consistently three feet off the ground. The original ice wagons, pulled by mules, were all that standard height. As time went by, ice plants slowly replaced their fleet of mules with "motor delivery equipment" but the necessary height of the platform remained the same. Those new trucks and later the standard pickup trucks had the same rear loading height as the original ice wagons. Decades down the road, larger delivery trucks and eighteen-wheeler tractor-trailers backed up to the same platforms to load and unload their cargo but their rear loading height was about a foot and half taller than the old platforms. Many plants adapted using a wooden ramp with rollers in the center to push the heavy blocks into the hauling trucks. Some plants opted for a chain-driven ramp to load the taller trucks.

For most ice customers, their main encounter with an ice plant was at the platform. There they saw the scoring machine, maybe the crusher, but definitely they found the icemen wielding massive cakes of crystal clear ice. People would line up at the platform, waiting with great anticipation for what the block ice would bring into their lives: maybe homemade ice cream after a huge family meal of fried chicken, ham, green beans, rice, black-eyed peas, probably some greens, homemade biscuits or cornbread, homemade blackberry cobbler and a three-layer chocolate cake with a deep fissure running through the middle signifying failure to our grandmothers but pure heavenly perfection to the rest of the world. Maybe they got one of the heavily-advertised "Iced Cold Watermelons" off the platform, picking out exactly the right floating, stripped melon from a deep bin filled with unimaginably frigid water. Or maybe they were getting a couple of partial blocks for a fishing outing with their grandchildren, sandwiches made at home, some sweet tea in a thermos, confident the ice in one cooler would keep lunch cool and fresh until everyone was starving from all the paddling and fishing and ice in another cooler would keep the bream or bass fresh until it was dressed on the backdoor stoop.

For a six-year-old child, the platform is nothing short of a stage. My cousin, a beautiful child and now a beautiful woman, would prance the length of the platform to the delight of the workers on their breaks. They coached her every time, "Now, whatcha gonna say when they crown you Miss America?" She would pivot at the end of the platform, wave a perfect queen's wave, flash her still-existent beauty queen's smile and say in her deep, slow, Southern drawl, "Hi Mississippi." Thirty-five years later, every Morris Ice Company worker I interviewed mentioned this silliness with tears of laughter in his eyes.

Interior of scoring machine, Scott's Ice Company; Thickness of storage room door, Hazlehurst Ice Company; Covered platform, MICO.

Rear view of storage room, MICO.

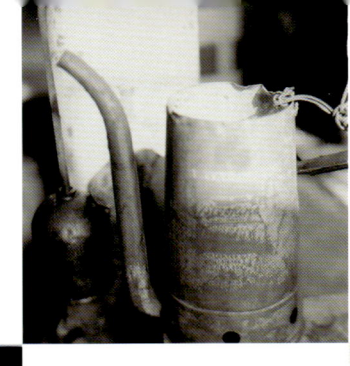

CHIP OFF THE OLD BLOCK

While researching for this book at the headquarters of *Refrigeration*, I was given a copy of their bicentennial issue, which featured histories of many of the long-running businesses in the field. I read every article and every ad, finding lots of useful information and hilarious tidbits. As I flipped through the classified section

in the back, I found a small ad that sought a restored/restorable horse-drawn ice wagon. "Call Pete," it said. It took me a year, but finally I called Pete; by then, he no longer worked at that number. I told the secretary I wanted to know if Pete had found a horse-drawn wagon. Not, I was quick to inform her, that I myself had one for sale, but that I was hoping he had bought one so I could get a photograph of the jewel. She didn't know but she told me Pete's daughter, who was out that day, would be able to help me if I could call back the next day. I got in touch with Kathy Barth, his daughter, and told her I was writing a book about block ice. I told her I had some old photos of buildings with mule-drawn wagons in the foreground, but the images were faded and too distant to show the details of a wagon. I asked if she knew if Pete had ever found a wagon. She wasn't sure which ad I was talking about, but she said her dad could help me out and asked whether I wanted his phone number or his address. I opted for his address and sent him one of the homemade brochures outlining my project with a letter inquiring about the chance to take a photograph of his ice wagon for the book. I was leery of the outcome, considering I'd spoken with two people who couldn't tell me if the man had a wagon or not. I thought, how hard is it to know if he has a huge old wagon or if there isn't one out in the garage? Man! The joke was entirely on me.

Pete Stack has so many ice wagons, ice trucks, iceboxes and so much ice memorabilia I understood, after visiting his collection, that the people I spoke with weren't trying to figure out if, but when, Pete had last purchased an ice-delivery vehicle. Only Pete could keep up with the inventory of his collection, located in a back warehouse of one of the most modern, fully automated ice factories in the nation, Brandywine Ice Company. For twenty years, Pete had owned, but had recently sold, this ice business near Philadelphia, Pennsylvania. It never was a block manufacturing plant but his father, John F. Stack, starting at age thirteen, in 1916, had his own team of horses and a wagon for his natural ice trade in New York. He was a good Irish Catholic man with a third-grade education from a family of nine. He cut pond and lake ice until he switched to selling manufactured ice in the mid-1940s.

This family exposure gave Pete a deep-seated passion for the entire history of block ice, both natural and manufactured. While I was gathering photographs to document the history of the block ice business, Pete was gathering, for years and years, every ice tool in every variation he could find. I focused my research on the machinery and blocks of ice; Pete acquired consumer memorabilia. While I was stomping through the weeds, looking for even a concrete foundation of a plant, Pete was stripping, dismantling, reconstructing, casting and rebuilding "best of show" antique 18th- and early 19th-century wagons and trucks. I lived at an ice plant, and Pete is opening a museum to share his collection, surely the largest in the country. I find the massive machinery from the block era enthralling. I cannot get enough of the abstract beauty of the actual blocks of ice, which always hurt if you touch them too long, no matter if the day is ninety-five degrees or hotter.

Pete knows about double clutch trucks. He knows the last body ever built for an ice truck was in 1947. He knows the icemen used the hole on the side of the truck to peek around the corner to see if anyone was coming. My manufacturing interests are not what most people know or remember about the block ice era. Smaller, more tangible objects trigger their memory, like the ones Pete has. A pair of tongs is about as iconic of the ice industry as there is, but who knew there were so many different types of tongs and that each major city in the Northeast

Pete Stack, with daughter Kathy Barth, in front of photo of Pete's father, John F. Stack.

had its own distinctive style? I knew ice picks were given out to customers, but only those privy to Pete's collection have ever seen 200 different ice picks at one time. Pete has at least one, often 500, of every tool used to refashion, resize, move, distribute, deliver and indulge in ice.

Like the machinery, these tools were crafted with great pride during the era before anyone had invented the despicable phrase "bottom line economics." Tools were made as best as one could make them, using the best materials, employing very talented individuals to hand-design the pieces, overseeing them from beginning to end. Profit—begging your pardon, greed—was not the purpose of production. Sure, people made very good livings in the block ice business, but they did so with honesty and integrity, satisfying a genuine need for comfort and convenience without sacrificing their principles. Tools were cast, not roboted together. Quality was inherent, not an ad campaign, because men depended on the tools for their living and scarcely were they let down. When the nut on a compressor weighs five pounds, is eight inches in diameter and two inches thick, you better have one heck of a wrench to fasten that thing down. Today, the used, discarded old equipment is still cherished by the iceman even though he must ply his own elbow grease to make the tools shine and function. Fortunately, for those with less time on their hands, there are honest workers making a living in the twenty-first century supplying items built to earlier standards.

Ever heard anyone say, "You're just a chip off the old block"? That expression was first recorded when Mr. Gothen, in 1920 at a Southern Ice Exchange convention, was talking about Theodore S. Behre, son of Charles H. Behre, of Pelican Ice Company of New Orleans, but it certainly applies to the machinery and tools in the business as well. All of the old equipment, from the massive engines down to the delicate dovetailed wooden boxes, is worthy of preservation.

Part of Pete's collection includes the equivalent of the homeowner's ice storage room, the treasured icebox. Today we value them as family heirlooms but they were an indispensable part of the home for many decades. It was one of the very first pieces of furniture newlyweds received or purchased when they started setting up house. An advertisement in *Good Housekeeping* states, "Fortunate, indeed, is the bride who starts housekeeping with a good ice refrigerator." For those of us who have survived out of dorm refrigerators the better part of our lives, such a necessity doubles the value of the box. Helen LaPlante, of Mexico Beach, Florida, remembers her mom gave her a stove for her wedding present, and the first thing she and her husband, Bob, purchased was an icebox. They got married in 1944, right after they got out of the service, and iceboxes were hard to come by. The Office of Price Administration, (OPA), established to prevent wartime inflation, set the price on iceboxes and rationed the number sold. Luckily, Mr. LaPlante knew someone who helped pull some strings so the newlyweds didn't have to go too long without a means for keeping fresh food in their home. Regrettably, the LaPlantes moved too many times over the years to keep up with the old icebox so she isn't one of the lucky ones who managed to transfer the icebox out of the kitchen and into the living room.

Photo courtesy Thomas Behmke

Pete, of course, has been fortunate enough to finagle an icebox or two into his living room, dining room, spare bedroom, and even some in the garage. The one

(clockwise) Decorative oak icebox; Detail of typical icebox; Open doors revealing lining of icebox. (right) Ice picks, Pete Stack collection.

Pete Stack collection, West Chester, Pennsylvania.

in his foyer ranks as the most unusual, elaborate icebox I saw during my journeys across ten southern and mid-Atlantic states. Made of solid oak, it has intricate carvings along the front panels and fancy claw feet for the upright box. Oak was the most popular wood used for iceboxes but most of the boxes had straight simple lines. The interior of all boxes was insulated with sawdust or seaweed then lined with tin or zinc. Many rural people couldn't afford any style of icebox so they used the earth as the icebox proper then lined the pit they'd dug in the ground with moss and sawdust. With just a little bit of ambition, they could also make an individualized-sized ice storage room out of thick wooden boards then keep it cool under the shade of the backyard oak tree. Often, people put yesterday's newspaper around the ice, believing it would help make the block last longer. Some iceboxes looked like our modern refrigerators with a compartment at the top for the block and a lower compartment for racks where the food was kept. Others had the block in the rear of the box with the food in front. Another unusual icebox in Pete's collection came with a separate side compartment for a small block of ice, not insulated as well, with a spigot to get an instant cold drink of melted ice water.

Whether the icebox cost a bunch of money or not, there was no getting around the need for a pan resting on the floor underneath it to catch the melting ice. The pan needed to be emptied daily—when you remembered. Mildred Behmke, of Mexico Beach, Florida, and her husband were a young newlywed couple in 1942, living in a second floor apartment. They were going out for a Saturday evening movie show. On the way there, she asked him "Did you…?" and before she could finish, he remembered it himself, replying "No. Didn't you?" The biggest problem with their predicament of an overflowing catch pan was where they lived—right above the landlord. They knew the catch pan for the icebox was close to full already and probably would be brimming over by the time they got home from the movie. The pans had a curved lip on them causing the water to fill over the pan by a quarter inch so if you even touched the pan, it would overflow. They were worried the landlord would say, "Look at what you kids did again." When the couple returned from their Saturday night outing, they squatted down on their hands and knees, and with two straws they sucked the water down below the rim to keep from dousing the landlord below. Everything in those days required some kind of fiddling with hands-on effort and the overflowing catch pan was certainly on the list of daily chores.

Leather delivery bag, Pete Stack collection.

In the South, we had iceboxes. In the North, they had ice chests and iceboxes. For the summertime, they used an ice chest, a freestanding wooden container. In the wintertime, there was no need to order delivered ice with the outdoor temperature already below freezing. They would stick a tin or metal container out the window to absorb the cold air, looking much like a modern window air conditioning unit, and the food went inside the freezing box. Children would always get corrected by their parents, saying, "That one in the window is an icebox, not an ice chest."

One of the nicest things about storing food in an icebox was how well the food lasted. Ice wasn't simply keeping the box cold, it was frozen water and as such, it added precious moisture, like having your own spray mister inside the refrigerator. Perhaps in the future the home refrigerator produce bins will be equipped with a tiny, self-regulating precipitation machine like is now so popular in the modern grocery stores. As refrigerators, the "celebrated mechanical devices," became more and more popular, there was a certain crowd that preferred their old icebox. Part of the attraction might have been how quiet the icebox was compared to the new, noisy, mechanical refrigerator, the home's first constant background hum. An ad in *The Red Book* magazine (*Redbook* since 1951) reveals a more glamorous reason why housewives kept their iceboxes, stating they took pride in the "savor and flavor to ice-freshened foods that husbands and guests are quick to notice and appreciate." Official posturing suggested iceboxes had an additional selling point, that melting ice carried odors out of the storage box so a block of cheese didn't end up absorbing the smell of its neighboring pot of turkey soup, but I got a few scoffs when I asked icebox users if this were indeed a valuable asset of the old oak storage containers. In truth, they had no idea what I was talking about.

The most symbolic item from the old block ice era must surely be the ice pick, used by icemen and lay workers alike. The picks came in a variety of sizes and shapes but each and every one was practical, functional, lightweight, and potentially dangerous for the uncoordinated. Ice plants put their logos on the picks and handed them out to customers along delivery routes, a good advertising ploy even when business was booming. These old ice picks are now coveted family keepsakes and draw pretty good money at a flea market or an antique store. The old ice saws, so distinctive with the big wide grin, also fetch a pretty penny when they surface for sale. Leather tote bags, once the lifesaver of the ice deliveryman, are hip new fashion accessories for trendy urbanities, according to the January 18, 2006, issue of the *New York Times* magazine. The small leather change purses, slung on the belt of the ice deliveryman, are very rare, but they still make an excellent wallet eliciting comments in grocery store lines.

Who knows where all the old artifacts are today, buried in the ground or tossed into landfills? Most of the plants have been razed, built over or left to that great Southern equalizer, kudzu, our arch nemesis capable of growing one foot per day, growing over the walls of abandoned factories, creeping across the floors and claiming untold numbers of accoutrements in its leafy wake. The block ice heritage is also being sold to foreign markets whose economics still warrant the labor-intensive block ice manufacturing business. In the United States, a block of ice sells for $7 and an ice puller makes $6 an hour. In Jamaica, workers make $100 a month, putting in twelve-hour shifts, seven days a week, plus there are no benefits, overtime and labor unions. The price of the ice is nearly equal in both places, but the demand for block ice is still quite high in the Caribbean, Mexico, and Central and South America. Wise businessmen from these areas come to the United States, purchase a block plant, lock, stock and barrel, for export back to their homeland. It's a good deal for the two businessmen, but the American public deserves the chance to value and experience this part of our heritage. So, here's to you, Pete, and to your intention to buy an old stone barn where you can open an antique ice museum, thus sharing and preserving the secrets of tools from long ago.

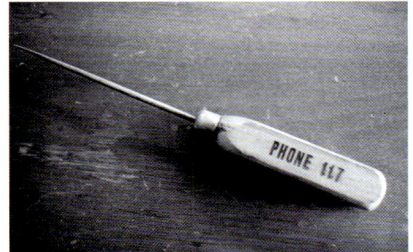

MICO ice pick.

HOMETOWN MEMORIES

The delicious cadence Southerners use for telling stories captured my imagination when I was an adult living in Jackson, Mississippi, and interacting with old friends of my family. I wanted, word for word, the tales I knew I'd hear from well-trained spinners to be an essential part of the documentation of the block ice era.

During my first trip to Mississippi in August, I felt fully prepared with a notebook and tape recorder handy during each interview. Back home, with all the notes and tapes spread out before me, I soon discovered only Uncle Remus' creator could translate oral stories into the written word. My silly little tape recorder had not captured the nuances of two women, same age, same employer, different races, different education, simultaneously answering my questions about the same person, their small-town ice deliveryman. The fortuitous interview with the women had offered a firsthand experience about life in the South: One woman was happy to remember that time in her life; the other woman was proud to tell me about it. One woman laughed with each new memory; the other woman stood taller as she watched me take notes. One of them had a job to pass the time of day; the other woman still put her paycheck toward rent.

They were friends as much as two people from such different positions in a closed environment can be. The women were trying so hard to give me all the help they could, making fun of their feeble memories due to their ages. Out of questions, I left the women to their task of Welcome Center hostess and assistant, chatting amongst themselves about all their good times as children when block ice was brought right to their homes—one thing the two races of the South shared. Although the women's familiarity with "Chilly Willie" depended on their parent's interests in the man or just the man's business hours, the ice deliveryman was a unifying factor during the Southern culture of yesteryear.

Draped in crisp, white clothes, the ice deliveryman was such a welcome sight he generally became famous around town, especially along his own delivery route. His was a hard job, though, physically demanding, having to lift blocks of ice all day long. Prior to the invention of the scoring machine in 1920, icemen relied on their tongs as a measuring device. Placed on the top of a block, the length of the tongs indicated a one hundred-pound section. He'd draw a line across the ice at the right height then chop away with his ice pick until he had one one-hundred-pound and one two-hundred-pound chunk of ice. Caught in a pinch, icemen continued to rely on their tongs for sizing but once scoring machines became a mainstay at ice plants, the deliveryman's first job of the day was to drag each 300-pound block of ice into the machine. Then, using his tongs, he'd drag the scored blocks onto the wagon or truck at the platform.

At every stop on his route he would find out how much the customer needed, either by word of mouth or from a square, ten-inch by ten-inch card placed in a window at the front of the house. The cards, given away by all ice plants, had "25 lb," "50 lb," "75 lb," "100 lb" printed on each quarter section of the card. If the housewife needed only seventy-five pounds that day, she'd put the card in her window so that "75 lb" was on the top and the deliveryman would know to bring in that much ice without having to make an extra trip. To take the ice inside, he had to load the ice into a canvas bag with a metal handle, hoist it onto his back, and carry it into the home, sometimes having to hike up stairs to a second- or third-floor apartment. Most homes had no locks on the doors so he'd go right in and take his melting cargo to the kitchen where, supposedly, all he had to do was put the block in the box. More likely

(opposite) Cast-iron toy wagon, M&M Ice and Cold Storage; (above) Delivery cards, Pete Stack collection.

Man carrying 400-pound block; Cristina Ice Company, Gretna, Louisiana, circa 1947.

than not, he had to do a lot of rearranging of condiment jars, fruits, meat and vegetables to make a space for the new block, no matter if the box had a "separate" compartment just for the ice. Once he made space for the new block of ice, he had to attempt to escape from the housewife who was always trying to take advantage of the able-bodied iceman. She would implore him to move a big chair or something else too heavy for her to maneuver, and she might need him to take out the trash for her. Or, she might be a good cook, so the iceman would intentionally linger around, waiting to enjoy his home-cooked breakfast at that stop. My grandmother, Corinne Morris, a.k.a. Bigmama to her grandchildren, slowed down the ice deliveryman with every visit he made. With one of the largest home iceboxes I heard of, holding three one hundred-pound blocks of ice, the deliveryman had a bit of a sloppy mess by the time he tromped in with so much ice. The cook, already taxed from keeping that behemoth icebox loaded to bear with homemade goodies just in case some hungry visitor might stop by, was not bothered at all by the mess the iceman made. In fact, it worked in her favor since it fell on his shoulders to clean up the wet ice trail, which in turn meant she never had to mop the kitchen floor.

The pages of the old trade journals are filled with constant complaints from the factories about the demands of housewives slowing up the workers, causing great trouble for the ice deliveryman and for his boss, forcing the price of ice to rise. Ad campaigns tried to educate the housewife, who pulled all the strings at home back in the time when no women nor men moved out of the home until they got married, reminding her that her lack of punctuality directly affected her own price for ice. Forty to fifty percent of the total operating expense of the ice company in the 1910s and 1920s went to the delivery alone, but household delivery was probably the greatest source of income then as well. The milk and laundry businesses managed to convert the housewife to accept all day deliveries, instead of just morning. The icemen wanted to do the same and to eliminate Sunday deliveries, but they were not so successful. The housewife was just too dependent on ice for everything in her kitchen, not like the one or two items the other businesses provided.

Most iceboxes, whether they took fifty-, seventy-five- or one hundred-pound blocks, needed a new block every two to three days. Ice plants had coupon books for the housewife, bought from the plant or the deliveryman, as a way of having prepaid sales. If the housewife got a fifty-pound block, the deliveryman would tear out two twenty-five-pound coupons. The driver would return to the plant at the end of the day with a packet of coupons, good only for that ice company. The coupon books also helped cut down on robberies.

Coupon book, MICO.

Since ice factories were happening places with so much business, they became targets for armed gunmen in need of some instant cash. In the 1920s these headlines reveal the need for caution: "Reports of robbers holding bookkeepers" and "A 2-ton truck was recently stolen from the lot of the Atlantic Ice Co."

As time went by and crushed ice became very popular, the iceman might have to take a block of ice and load it into a crusher sitting on the back of his truck. These machines were fashioned a bit differently from the crushers at the ice plants. Revolving drums with picks spun rapidly, liable to catch anything nearby. When the iceman

City Products Corporation ad.

loaded a block, he had to be careful or the crusher would catch the tongs and pull them down into the machine, leaving hands and arms dangerously close to being crushed and pulverized. That job eased off a bit when plants completely made the transition to "bagged, block or blown" ice but for a while, the deliveryman needed to be both strong and cautious.

While out on his route, the ice deliveryman would have a string of children, particularly in the summertime, running behind his ice truck. An in-town deliveryman for the Morris Ice Company, "Mr. Chill," born Nathaniel Sandifer, laughed fondly when he recalled all the little children and how they loved trying to see if they could get a sliver of ice to suck on like a popsicle or to get some ice to put in a glass of lemonade, which made it so cold it hurt your teeth to drink it. If he didn't have some crushed ice, he'd be called bad names, and all the kids would be after him! If the kids managed to wangle some ice, the mom might come out with a bowl or a cup asking, "Can you give me some? You'll be back tomorrow?" Then someone else would be out with a glass, "I want some ice!"

This same nostalgic man complained every day in his twenties about his backbreaking job, his bleeding shins and black-and-blue thumbs. Every day, he told his boss man, James "Mr. Jobie" D. Harris, he was going to quit the job. Mr. Jobie was a smooth talker and always promised Sandifer he'd get better at moving the ice around, the job would get easier, to keep the faith and come back the next day. Initially, payday is what really kept him coming back, thinking he'd make it until Friday when he was going to quit for sure. But having his own route with customers who called him "Mr. Chill" and "Cool Breeze" and were so happy to see him, he soften on the job and managed to stick it out—for forty more years!

Working on a daily basis with the public, being in and out of people's homes and supplying businesses with a needed commodity, ice deliverymen really had to be friendly and most were the entertaining sort. Sandifer, who had the gift of gab, created a loyal fan base, telling tall tales or playing tricks down at the ice plant. He loved to tease customers with his ability to hide dry ice in his mouth without burning his tongue and blow the smoke out while he held an unlit cigarette in his hand. But at times, he was confronted with some strange occurrences at his routine stops. There was the scary moment he entered the Hat and Cane Club, a beer joint off Gallatin Street, to deliver ice to a regular customer when the dark room suddenly lit up from the flare of a gun being shot. Sandifer wasn't hurt, nor was anything else except the adjacent doorknob, but it was a few days before he returned to that customer with a load of ice. He related another incident, the tale coming to life with sprinkles of his laughter, his dramatic pauses filling his audience with anticipation. "Well,…" Sandifer says, "this lady I had on my regular route, you see, she calls me up one day…" Switching to a terrible high-pitched voice, he continues, "'Sandifer', she says, 'I needs some ice. I'm having a get-together this weekend so I needs you to come….'" Sandifer obliges, and loads up a canvas bag with one hundred pounds of crushed ice. He says, "I goes up the steps, it was an upstairs house, and so I went in the kitchen as usual. I gets in there and soon I went to back around to the table, you know, let it ease off my shoulder." The lady has "one of them yapping dogs with the squashed-up face" who knows Sandifer but the dog always yips, startling him when he delivers the ice. Sandifer continues, "This little old dog nipped me before I could unload the bag. I let that whole hundred pounds of ice go." It falls to the floor with the tiniest sound of muffled air. The lady comes in, and starts screaming, "You done killed my dog! You killed my dog!" Sandifer's eyes bug out; he looks at her, at the dog under the sack of ice, at the woman again and he leaves right then, leaving the canvas bag there on the floor. "She called asking for me to come back," Sandifer says. "She didn't have no hard feelin's. It took me awhile before I'd go back up there, but eventually I did."

A different deliveryman, in Friars Point, Mississippi, called in sick for work one day, but volunteered his son to cover his delivery route. The young man knew how to drive an ice truck so he went to the factory, got a load of ice, and delivered the blocks to all his dad's

Nathaniel "Cool Breeze" Sandifer, former MICO ice deliveryman.

customers. When he got back to the plant, one lady had called, asking for her ice. The young man told Mr. A. C. "Buck" Arenz, the plant manager, he'd delivered that lady her ice. "Well," Mr. Arenz said, "She can't find it and she says she didn't get any ice. Let's go back over to her house and you show her where the ice is." Turns out, the young man had indeed given the woman a block of ice and it was sitting right where he left it, not in the curious new item called an icebox, but in a similarly shaped item, the woman's oven!

The ice deliveryman was a warm and wonderful part of the block ice era. He represented so much joy and ease for so many people. James Wilson, United States Secretary of Agriculture in 1920 declared, "It is a blessing to be able to put meat, vegetables and fruit into cold storage where they will keep, there is no doubt about that." Unofficially, ice hit home in more intimate ways. Many of the ice customers I interviewed said people from the electrical age could never imagine how delicious it was to have a sip of cold sweet tea on Sundays when their moms would be extravagant, slivering off some ice for each child and serving the delicacy with the family meal. I often wonder if we have lost this concept of delicacies, with so much available at any time of day or night, any season of the year. One thing is for sure, back then, the saying "Ice makes life nice" was definitely true.

The ice wagons themselves helped proclaim the value of the iceman's product, becoming traveling billboards promoting the pleasures of ice. Each plant developed its own logo and style, some in carnival colors of bright reds and yellows, often with entertaining logos of a poplar bear wrapped in a scarf sitting next to a glacier, or penguins with happy, smiling faces—everything signaled that ice was part of a good time. The wagons were hand-painted with great pains taken with the lettering and the logos to attract attention on the streets. The iceman had a bell he rang, distinctive from the other deliverymen, to let his customers know he was in the neighborhood. In New Orleans, where Louis Armstrong was influenced by all the melodies of the men peddling their wares, the iceman had a song he sang that announced it was time for his customers to get their square ice cards out in the window so he could bring them some ice today—and not wait until tomorrow.

The wagons themselves were distinctive from other delivery wagons with two canopies, a regular one in the front and one in the rear where the iceman spent most of his time retrieving the ice. The wagons had to have excellent suspension to carry the heavy loads of block ice. The front wheels were smaller than the rear wheels, making maneuvering u-turns simple. The taller rear wheel kept the bed of the wagon at a comfortable height for the iceman to hoist the block of ice on his back for deliveries. Some wagons didn't even have a seat in the front for the driver. Instead, the iceman sat on the rear bench as the wagon moseyed along, then he hopped off and gathered his ice load when he was at the right stop. The mule in the front of the wagon was steering and driving the wagon. They were very intelligent, those mules. They knew exactly which houses on the route got ice and how long it took to deliver the right quantity of ice. It's conceivable that an ice deliveryman could have diddle-dawdled too long, lifting the dining room table so the housewife could get the carpet out for a good sweeping, only to discover the mule, with the wagon and all the ice, had headed on down the street of his own volition to the next house on the route!

Transportation costs for a wagon used a different standard of measurement than our modern trucks and cars. Instead of miles per gallon, the wagons operated on meal expenditures. In 1915, it cost an average of $10 or less a month to feed one mule. After World War I, it cost from $20-$28 according to the season. A mule that cost $225 went for $400 after the war and shoes were $2 versus $1 before. Icemen tackled such problems by asking, "Which draft animal do you prefer for ice delivery, horse or mule?"

1885 Knickerbocker ice delivery wagon,
Pete Stack collection;
Circa 1925 Hubley cast-iron toy ice wagon,
Pete Stack collection;
1910 ice wagon,
Pete Stack collection.

Old-fashioned water pump; *Ladies Home Journal* ad, produced by National Association of Ice Industries 1928©.

Like many ice plants, the Morris Ice Company chose a fleet of mules for the daily ice deliveries to homes and businesses. The mules lived in a barn on the property, creating the perfect conditions for rich, life-sustaining soil.

A living testament to this history of mules and ice wagons now graces the old barn site in the form of the Mississippi Champion Fig Tree. This history provides so great a source of fertilizer, the ground seems resilient to depleting its concentration because the deeper the fig tree grows its roots, the more proficient is its circumference and the more luscious its fruit. Come August, during fig harvesting time, my uncle Hebron places a small sign by the tree, discouraging passersby from partaking in the tree's delicacy. He has enough of a fight on his hands with the birds, which apparently prefer figs far less ripe than we humans do. One summer before I lived at the plant Hebron suckered me into canning some figs. Hebron, Ben, an all-around fix-it man, and I picked the fruit from the tree and I used my sister's kitchen to turn them into preserves. The end product was quite delicious, mostly in thanks to a countrywoman who graciously shared her secret recipe when she heard of our endeavor. You can pretty much guarantee that modern transportation residue—gasoline spills, oil changes and used tires—will never create an environment that can produce food fit for the gods.

As long as mules and horses were the engines for the wagons, ice delivery remained an in-town event. At their clippety-clop speed, there wouldn't be much ice left by the time the iceman arrived at his destination if he took his wares too far out of town. Farmers, an ingenious bunch unaccustomed to sitting around waiting on someone else to help them out, pooled their resources to get some of the wonderful coolness of ice for themselves. Each Saturday, during the weekly trip into town, someone took their turn at getting as much ice as possible for the neighboring farmers. Their determination accounts for much of the increased consumption of ice during the late 1910s. By the 1920s, it was a standard sight in cities and on farms ten to fifteen miles in the country to see people enjoying an iced cold drink.

That cold drink was certainly a welcome luxury in a lifestyle dependent on the sweat of one's brow. The country table was set with food that had been planted, grown, fattened, cut, killed and processed right there by the family. Wood stoves, with no temperature control devices, just "low, middlin' and hot," were the order of the day, well up into the 1930s and early 1940s on southern farms. There were two stoves usually, one inside the home for winter use and an outdoor one used during summer cooking to keep the home free of extra heat. The icebox, sitting in the kitchen or out on the porch in the shade, not only kept butter firm and hard, the buttermilk cool, and the cabbage slaw crisp, it relinquished time constraints for when food had to be consumed or purchased, resulting in a happier housewife and a happier household. The freedoms that came with the icebox made such an impression on my maternal, pastoral grandmother, Maggie Price, she remained ever-thankful every Saturday of her life that she could cook her homemade Sunday dinner one day in advance and safely keep the meal under ice until guests arrived the following day. When the fifteen to twenty hungry family and friends showed up, she relaxed with them, enjoying their company, and breathed easier knowing her house wasn't sweltering from the heat of the oven.

Mamo Price's life, like many other southerners' lives, had been a simple one. Until President Franklin Delano Roosevelt created the Rural Electrification Administration in 1935, country folks had no electric lines. The early business slogan for ice factories may have been "Write Wire Phone," but the average country customer was far from living such an extravagant lifestyle. When darkness came, they used candles for evening lights. Their water wasn't out of a tap but came from priming an outdoor pump by hand. An anonymous friend, who grew up in the late 1920s, early 1930s, confided a humorous memory about growing up on a farm without electricity or indoor plumbing, just an outhouse in the backyard. "You hear about it," she said, "and we really did use the Sears catalog for paper. I would use only the pages with nighties and soft images. I'd never use a page with a stove or something hard. It's funny what you do as a kid."

W.C. "Sonny" Fortner, Jr., the owner of Scott's Ice Company in Anguilla, Mississippi, tried in the 1990s to get the Mississippi Agricultural Museum to put his miniature, ten-ton a day, ice plant next to the museum's replica of a 1930s kitchen. The commission turned him down, saying ice was manufacturing, rather than agriculture. Nonetheless, ice was one of the most important and treasured items in the kitchen, defining when and what the family ate for their everyday meals.

Kerosene brake light on 1928 Mac AC ice truck, Pete Stack collection; 1928 Mac AC five-and-a-half-ton ice truck, Pete Stack collection.

Once people like my maternal grandmother were hooked on the wonders of ice, plants could be profitable out in small, rural towns. These remote municipalities jumped at the chance to have a near-by ice plant, constructing their own ice factories during the 1920s, 1930s and 1940s. At the same time, mules and horses gave way to private motorcars and new motorized delivery trucks. The trucks, zooming faster down the road than the four-legged beast of burdens had trotted, greatly reduced the delivery times for the iceman, albeit the driver now had no choice but to steer his own vehicle. This new fleet of Ford or International trucks enabled the iceman to begin servicing regular country routes. In 1938, fifty cents would bring an ice deliveryman out to the country once a week in his Ford truck filled with blocks of ice. People who lived deep in the woods still had to drive to town to get ice, as a delivery route was only profitable if neighbors lived nearby.

The new fleet of machines had one drawback—they were a bit more volatile than the old animals. According to Joe Monaco, a restoration expert working for Pete Stack at Brandywine Ice Company, they were "moving time bombs" from the many different ignitable fuels on board. The truck engines ran on gasoline. The headlights ran on kerosene, or "coal oil" as the country folks called it. The lights by the cab used their own tank of propane, which rode alongside the running board of the driver. Fortunately, there were few accidents and no one drove the fast speeds of today so the fuel containers weren't likely to explode. City dwellers also benefited from the invention of the combustion engine, which enabled self-service in between their regular deliveries. The early automobiles were perfect for small ice pick-up with their running boards doubling as ice carriers; they kept the dripping water out of the interior of the beautiful 1920 Model T.

The melting ice was no problem for the new trucks, just as the wagons had been well prepared for their load. The beds were made of cypress or oak to handle the inevitable moisture coming off exposed blocks of ice and to withstand the weight of the ice. Smaller bed trucks held about eight blocks across and five blocks deep, a heavy load at 12,000 pounds. One of the favorites amongst icemen, the International C ice truck, could carry sixteen upright blocks across and ten blocks deep for a total weight over 60,000 pounds. The rear wheels of an International truck were pulled with a chain, as opposed to the drive shaft that turns modern wheels, but they withstood the daily rounds for years and years. The new trucks were no longer covered like the old ice wagons had been. Once the deliveryman filled the bed for his daily route, he threw a thick, canvas tarp over the whole load. Off he'd go, the hotter the day, the faster he had to drive to keep from having a trail of water behind the truck. The trucks had no heater so in winter the driver would remove the doghouse, the floorboard covering the transmission, and that's where he'd get his heat. Now, the slower he went, the more heat he had. The heat made the windows fog up, so he'd have to carry a rag and wipe as he drove, but he'd get the day done and the ice delivered. Even in those trucks, a quarter the size of a modern eighteen-wheeler, he really had to know how to drive an ever-changing, slippery, melting load that acted as a mass, or not, depending on how long the blocks had been on the truck. It was always a challenge to drive well enough to keep the load from throwing the truck in the ditch. A couple of men lost their lives driving a load of ice from the Morris Ice Company in Jackson one hundred miles over to the nuclear power plant in Port Gibson, Mississippi. They worked for the power company, not the ice plant, and were not familiar with how a load of ice can slide around, throwing the truck over at a sharp curve.

The ice trucks had a distinctive "clock clock clock" sound, even as late as the 1960s, that could be heard two blocks away. It was a great sound to David Gautier in Pascagoula, Mississippi, during his salad days in elementary school, as he would always interrupt the class, exclaiming, "That's my dad's truck, that's my dad's ice truck." All the students could hear what was happening outside through the open windows of the elementary school. Like almost all the other Southern schools in the early 1960s, they had no air conditioning. Electric fans stood in one corner of the room, oscillating across sweltering children who may or may not be able to concentrate on anything other than the heat—and the longing for just one sliver of ice out the back of

David's dad's passing ice truck. The Pascagoula Ice and Freezer trucks were on their way to commercial businesses or delivering ice to the many poor people still in the area using an icebox as their only means of refrigeration.

For many businesses and homeowners, there was a middleman iceman. The peddler would arrive early in the morning at the ice plant, pick up ice using his own wagon or truck, and head out to make his daily sales. The peddlers were able to service people who didn't have any means to get to the plant or were simply not serviced by the regular iceman. In large cities and in smaller towns, the peddler market was a big part of business at the ice plant, especially in the summer. The peddler often cut a deal with the iceman, who made some money but didn't have to take on the expenses of delivering ice. Many a peddler went on to bigger things, some of them even became bank presidents.

Always keeping up with the needs and demands of modern lifestyles, block ice businesses diversified their deliveries, shifting exclusively from home delivery to new markets made available by the growing number of automobiles and the new types of businesses open to serve the ever-mobile population. High on the list of new businesses was the "grocery store," a place where a multiplicity of items was sold under one roof. At one of these newfangled businesses, the housewife could purchase "upon the cash and carry plan" a number of her needs at one stop; she no longer had to go to the fruit distribution center at the railroad tracks to get her fresh produce or the meat market to get meat already cut up and wrapped in packages. While at the grocery store, she could also get her ice in small blocks or the store would chip up the ice and bag it for her. These grocery stores grew in popularity with the iceman because he could sell ice much more cheaply there than in home deliveries.

The next big delivery opportunity was the ice vending machine, placed near other businesses such as gas stations or grocery stores, where the machine delivered "ice at your fingertips" twenty-four hours a day. Via an "ice-a-teria," an automatic coin-operated conveyor-fed machine, anyone could purchase three different kinds of processed ice: by the bag, in ten-pound or twenty-five-pound blocks. The customer put coins in the machine, picked which size ice was desired, watched if a block was crushed and bagged, then saw it drop in the slot for removal. This new "self-serve" concept of curbside machines was a great success; by the end of WWII they were everywhere. In 1953, the ice business called City Products Corporation,

Door of 1945 Dodge ice delivery truck.

in St. Louis, Missouri, had thirty-six stations in the city and thirty more in the suburban areas. The vending station machines gave the iceman some trouble, breaking down too often, so those contraptions soon gave way to the ice merchandiser. Invented by Bill Rothe and Lee Rothe of Leer in 1952, the merchandiser is the outdoor box people are familiar with today. The clerks at the convenience stores really appreciated these new ice merchandiser boxes. These boxes come with their own cooling capabilities whereas before, stores without vending stations had to house blocks of ice in the walk-in cooler. When someone wanted a bag of ice, the clerk had to load one block at a time into a crusher and bag the ice. With the advent of self-cooling machines, all that responsibility shifted back to the iceman whose employees bagged ice at the plant, then the deliveryman would stock the merchandisers as part of his ice delivery route. At Crystal Ice Company, in Mobile, Alabama, Joe Quinlivan would sit at busy intersections in town with a thumb ticker in hand, counting the number of cars crossing during an hour. Wherever the people passed in great numbers, he set up an ice merchandiser for easy access, ending up with fifteen locations around town. One station alone, at a Pak-A-Sak store, was reloaded four times one July 4th. It must've been a hot one because that's close to four and a half tons of ice from one box at one location on one day! Even under normal summer circumstances, merchandisers consistently sold out of ice, the ice trucks returning during the day to restock the refrigerated containers.

Such were the daily adventures for the iceman and his fellow workers. Life with ice was never a routine, though, and plants had many requests to spice up numerous occasions. An annual extravaganza found at many Southern small towns was the use of ice as "snow," the natural product being a very rare and illusive occurrence down in the Gulf South States. Cities would splurge for fake snow for Christmas scenes, turning their town centers into picturesque winter wonderlands. Happy with the beautiful views, no one every complained that the iceman's snow wasn't fluffy and soft. Seeing how pretty the ice looked on the government property, regular citizens got the notion they could transform their own yards. Individuals with money to burn would call up the local ice plant, tell them they wanted to be the only ones in the neighborhood with a snowy winter scene for the holidays. Sometimes they would want a snowy front yard in the middle of summer! "How big is your yard?" the iceman would ask. "Oh, you can get by with fifteen blocks of ice." "Come on!" the ice fiend would say and off the ice truck went, covering their yard in snow made at the local ice plant. Ice plants up in the hill country on the northern edges of the Deep South supplied their own form of bells and whistles during the sweltering summer months. Fun-loving landowners would buy twenty blocks or more, throw them down on the ground together in a long pile and swoosh, they'd free-fall downhill on the slippery slope of blocks melted together, forming their very own super-slide. Women's magazines promoted the youthful rejuvenating effects of using ice as part of the beauty treatment for excessive dry or oily, mature skin, recommending aging women finish their nightly cleansing routine by covering their faces and throats with strips of wet, clean cotton then rubbing ice over the strips for two minutes. Joan Crawford took the bait, hoping ice would preserve her youthful appearance in the manner ice slowed food deterioration. James Bond, of Hollywood fame, always wanted his cocktail "Shaken, not stirred" because manufactured block ice, when shaken, splinters into super fine tiny ice crystals that chill each molecule of liquid in a drink without watering it down. Ice changed people's lives in so many ways!

(opposite) Twenty-four hour service station, M&M Ice and Cold Storage; (above) 1945 Dodge ice delivery truck, MICO.

UNSUNG HERO

Researching something that hasn't been researched before is hard to do when your normal areas of research—the library and the Internet—let you down. It's fascinating at the same time to go into a major university library, ask for information on the block ice era—seeking anything on manufactured ice—only to have

the librarian look back with a blank face. Such was my luck while at the University of Mississippi library, at Oxford, Mississippi. That information repository is no small joint so when the highly skilled woman standing in front of me offered not one word of response, I figured we were experiencing a nominal communication failure. I tried rewording the question, describing my need for anything written or any records that might show local or state information on block ice. More deadpan silence. Fortunately, most librarians are curious people and not inclined to give up on the first failure. Eventually, the librarian lead my boyfriend and me up the stairs to a section on state history where, as happened at most libraries around the South, we found one or two tidbits of raw data to help document the importance of the era. Sometimes, the eldest librarian on duty had more useful information in her head than was scattered amongst an entire collection of literary documents. Even the Internet has scant information on block ice. If you want natural ice, you will have to stand in line, and if you want air conditioning, you better bring a cozy chair for the litany of praise. Those topics have been recognized and re-recognized, but the record keepers have skipped over an industry that existed in just about every town in every state and is in the minds and hearts of everyone over the age of fifty-five. Baby boomers may not have known a local ice deliveryman but uttering the words "block ice" elicits a string of stories from most and even Gen-Xers know a thing or two about iceboxes and big blocks of ice.

The popular slogan, "His Majesty, the Iceman" tells it like it was: people everywhere across the nation, in private homes, in the public sector, and for commercial businesses, relied on the iceman's ice. Starting in 1845, when Dr. John Gorrie invented the world's first successful means at producing artificial coolness, block ice gained momentum year after year, steadily infiltrating its way in a dazzling array of enterprises. Perhaps the shear commonality of block ice has caused its phenomenal record to be ignored. Perhaps so many different factors helped steamroll the business into the daily lives of Americans that its history remained segmented and thick in mystery. Piece by piece, those events fueled the artificial ice business into one of great stature and renown.

One such event took place on July 29, 1881, affecting both the outcome of ice production and the health of the nation. Prior to this date, the Illinois Central Railroad, "Main Line of Mid-America," from Chicago to New Orleans, used two different sized railroad gauges. The northern gauge, from Cairo, Illinois, to Chicago, was the standard gauge of four feet eight and a half inches. The southern ICRR lines, formerly owned by the New Orleans, Jackson & Great Northern Railroad and the Mississippi Central Railroad Companies, used a wide gauge of five feet. This discrepancy in sizes meant the wheels on every freight car had to be changed out on each side of the Ohio River. That summer in 1881, beginning at dawn and finishing at 3 p.m., more than 30,000 men converted the entire 547-mile line from Cairo to New Orleans to standard gauge. This cut a 900-mile trip from seventy-two hours down to about fourteen or sixteen. It was an incredible breakthrough for the meat and produce industries throughout the South; it opened up the entire northern and mid-western markets to the bounty of the warm sub-tropical climates. As a result, production of fruits and vegetables rose in the South way out of proportion to the increase in population between 1890 and 1920. Regional areas of specialization, such as Georgia peaches, Florida oranges and Texas beef, began to form. Local items became regional foods and then national products because of the ease of transportation with a unified railroad system and inexpensive block ice, used on every trip to keep the perishables fresh and nutritious.

As the agriculture business boomed, construction of new ice plants

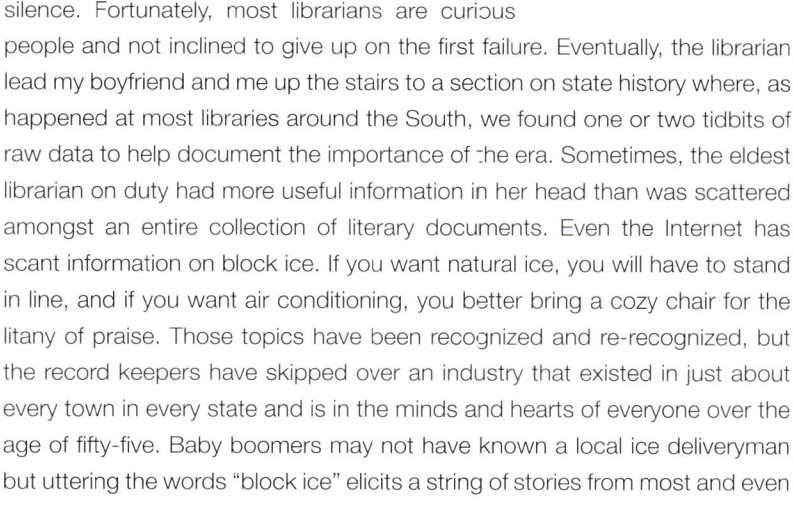

Hazlehurst Ice Company, Hazlehurst, Miss.

skyrocketed in Southern states. Trade magazines are filled with reports of construction of new plants in practically every small town across the South, the onslaught starting in the 1910s. Cities and towns without their own plants advertised for anyone to please come start a plant in their community. With so much available ice, new agricultural ventures heretofore unheard of in the South, such as poultry-raising and dairy farming, cropped up in the region and quickly became firmly established. The block business wasn't doing too shabbily throughout the rest of the country either. At the turn of the twentieth century mid-western and western states were catching on to the wonders of artificial ice just as northern businesses and homeowners were rapidly shifting from tainted harvested ice to manufactured ice. So many ice plants popped up everywhere that block ice gained complete command of the refrigeration needs of the entire nation.

On occasion, a new ice plant was not a welcome sight, at least not to the established plant owners who found competition a threatening proposition, as one entrepreneur quickly found out. Mr. James Quinlivan of Montgomery, Alabama, started a modest ice business in town in 1901. He no longer lived there by 1902 because he had been run out of town by the elite, old Southern-money families who ruled the Montgomery ice business and decided that no young whippersnapper was going to be allowed on their roost. Thinking he might have a better go of it on the Gulf Coast in Mobile, Alabama, Quinlivan built a plant, hired a couple of workers and opened his doors in May 1902 with a load of ice for sale. His new plant was on Front Street, beside a small triangle that held a sundry store of sorts. The day after he opened for business, the sundry store delved into a new line of merchandise, block ice, graciously and inexpensively supplied by the Good Old Boys club. They set the price for their ice at forty-five cents a pound, five cents less than their new neighbor. With only a painted sign for investment, Quinlivan quickly knocked down his price to forty cents. Ganging up on the newcomer, GOBs dropped their price to thirty-five cents. Quinlivan, counting his pennies, calculated he had enough money to last seven days, until Sunday, before he'd be out of business and completely bankrupt. If he was going out, he was going to do so with a bang, so he dropped his ice to ten cents a pound. Shocked, the GOBs figured anyone that had the guts to go that low on their price of ice must have some mighty big family money for backing, so very quietly, on Saturday, the sundry store took down its sign "Ice for Sale," and never sold another block of ice. Quinlivan's Crystal Ice Company thrived in that location where he, his son

Crystal Ice Company, circa 1905; Crystal Ice Company, Mobile, Ala.

and now his grandson, Steve Quinlivan, have continued to sell ice to the surrounding communities.

By the time World War I hit, the ice business was so important a man could be excused from war duty if he worked in an ice plant. Ice production didn't slow down once "The War" was over. Soldiers brought back tales of the varied customs they experienced during their deployment, which instigated new desires on the part of the American public. They wanted to go out to eat at restaurants instead of having home-cooked meals. Driving luxurious automobiles became a popular pastime. Both men and women wanted to be seen sashaying around in fancy clothing. Each of these desires increased the demand for manufactured ice. Restaurants needed it for food preservation and to serve iced cold drinks. Ice was used in concrete mixtures for new roads. The textile industry relied on block ice to control the temperature in their dye vats. All kinds of industrial development increased after the war and all of it, whether directly in making the product or just in supplying office workers with cold drinks, fed into the ice business.

Prosperity always attracts a crowd and those times in the South were no exception. As the South itself became more populated, the block ice industry became more firmly entrenched in its infrastructure. Not only were new plants going up, but existing plants were increasing their capital to meet the ever-increasing demand for ice. The Home Light and Ice Company in the small town of Cleveland, Mississippi, increased its capital from $10,000 to $40,000 in 1920. Leading capitalists were building, buying and amassing plants in their own states, neighboring states and across the country. Charles A. Zilker of Dallas, Texas, had been on the ice trail for a few decades when in 1928 he sold all his plants, from Texas to Atlanta to Pittsburgh, to the Samuel Insull Interests of Chicago for $1 million. That's 1928 dollars, a pretty penny for one of the cheapest, but most useful of that day's modern conveniences. In 1920, the industry added close to $1 billion a year to the wealth of the people of the United States and it ranked ninth in the amount of investment among American commercial enterprises. According to the U. S. Census Bureau 4,800 block ice plants employing 160,000 people produced forty million tons of ice in 1920, that's nearly 750,000 blocks of ice every twenty-four hours.

At the Southern Ice Exchange convention in 1922, icemen celebrated their remarkable exploits and their place in history. "The ice industry has became one of the most vital factors in the nation's development and the ice manufacturers have just reason for pride in their accomplishments," said President S. C. Oliver during his address. He assured them they ought "to feel a pardonable pride…in the widespread benefits which have resulted to the people of our country." In fact, he said, part of the ability of American cities to grow so rapidly in population during the twentieth century was "due to the dependable supply of farm products, since without iced refrigerator cars, the great cities would starve." The block ice industry was on an unstoppable roll, responding eloquently to the needs of the country and consistently being a driving force of creativity, ingenuity and passion.

Icemen, none of whom could ever be accused of being lazy, weren't the kind to settle on their laurels regardless of the instrumental impact their industry meted out on the culture of America. It is not an industry short of heroes rising to their calling. John Jefferson "Uncle Johnny" Green is one such iceman who drove the industry forward with his inventiveness and entrepreneurial spirit. In 1927, he was operating a small frame ice dock in Dallas, Texas. Uncle Johnny stayed open late all summer, usually putting in sixteen hours a day, every day of the week. His customers appreciated his long hours and some of them told Uncle Johnny how nice it would be if he had a few other items, like bread and eggs they could pick up on Sundays and in the evenings when the regular food markets were closed. Uncle Johnny, who was operating the ice dock for a newly-formed ice company, recognized a good opportunity when he saw one. He decided to finance this new endeavor with money out of his own pocket. Before the end of the summer, word had spread through the neighborhood about the food items for sale at Uncle Johnny's dock, and he had to add three new shelves to stock enough items to keep up with the demand. Uncle Johnny decided he didn't want to shut down the ice dock that winter in order to keep his sideline business going. He went to the offices of the new ice company and asked to speak to the head honcho, Mr. Jodie Thompson. Uncle Johnny said he'd pay the power bills if Mr. Thompson would supply the milk, bread, eggs, cigarettes and a few canned items. In the spring, Uncle Johnny said, he would come back to the office and settle up with the owner. This plan of having milk and eggs at the ice plant sounded odd to the young company official, but he had no reason to say no. He said go ahead and see what happens. The following spring, Uncle Johnny returned with $1,000 in cash, the ice company's share of Uncle Johnny's profits. Mr. Thompson was obviously impressed because all the company's ice plants soon began offering a few food items to be toted away. Other ice plants across the country adopted this business practice, but no one took the idea and ran with it like the Southland Ice Company—now better known as the inventor of the convenience store, the multi-billion dollar international corporation found right in your own neighborhood, the 7-11 stores. As their slogan states, "Oh, Thank Heaven for 7-11"—and Uncle Johnny and ice.

The following excerpt is from the February, 1930, issue of *Refrigeration*, four months after the stock market crash on Black Tuesday: "The Home and Ice Company of Tupelo, Mississippi, will double its capacity and work of enlarging the plant will be started immediately. The company

City Products Corporation ad showing workers blowing layers of crushed ice onto produce.

will spend $25,000 on the expansion. New compressors, new condensers and new tanks will be installed, bringing the daily output to 24 tons." During the heart of the Depression, in 1934, sixty-seven of eighty-two counties in Mississippi had ice plants with a value of $3,630,000, which closely matched the value of the industry prior to the beginning of the worldwide economic downturn. Across the country, the ice industry was hardly affected by the Great Depression, so dependent were Americans on ice. There were references in the trade magazines during this time about public unhappiness with the ice industry, claiming it had the public in the palm of its hand. It wasn't so much that the icemen took advantage of the situation by charging exorbitant prices, it was just that they sold such incredible quantities to the masses who had no alternative to meet their refrigeration needs.

Household consumption is the most commonly known application for block ice but the demand for ice by an array of commercial enterprises eventually far exceeded the demand of individual usage. Movie theaters, one of the first public places to air-condition entire rooms, were one of the most popular businesses using block ice. The brand new experience of walking into a cool room in the middle of the sweltering outdoor heat teased silver screen viewers as dramatically as the flickering lights. Imagine, had they not used ice for cooling, the discomfort of a dark room filled with one hundred hot bodies attempting to create coolness with nothing more than a hand-held paper fan. Imagine the thick humidity, the suffocating flat, dead air and the sweat slowly rolling down your spine, under your thighs and under your armpits down your rib cage. Saturday afternoon matinees would never have been the exotic memories of an entire generation without the delicious coolness and comfort of block ice. Every Saturday and Sunday, Morris Ice Company deliveryman Nathaniel Sandifer switched his route from the chicken plants to drive past the long lines of teenagers waiting for tickets to the newest show. The one he remembers best, "Love Me Tender," had a line around the building, but he and his ice delivery were so appreciated by the movie house that "Cool Breeze" got the very first ticket to the show. Most theaters used the basic method Dr. John Gorrie had employed for his fever patients—some ice and a fan—but others, like the famous Orpheum Theater in New Orleans, Louisiana, used an elaborate ice cooling system whose grand scale filled the entire basement. The theaters also served refreshing cold drinks, using shaved ice for their soda fountain drinks.

Block ice continued to be a viable industry after World War II, attractive to a new round of adventurous businessmen. Their incentive wasn't just the profits available from a steady income, but also the inexpensive means suddenly available for starting up an ice plant. With the second worldwide conflict at an end, the military no longer needed the block ice equipment used during the war effort so they unloaded it on a crowd of eager capitalists. Buying surplus stock at public auction was a great way to get machinery at reasonable rates. One of the nine ice plants in Jackson, Mississippi, the well-known Jac Mac Ice Company, started with military surplus and sold ice made with that equipment for thirty years. The Morris Ice Company added a long wing to our family plant when we purchased leftover war stock and it remained in service for the company for the next twenty-five years. The ice-storage room built for this new wing became my photography darkroom while I lived at the plant, further extending the life of the investment into the following century.

In New Orleans, Louisiana, a glut in the ice market produced by military surplus equipment resulted in a big ice war. Behind closed doors in the Big Easy, charismatic icemen formed an association, and they successfully convinced all the local ice plants to join. Unlike reputable ice associations across the country, this one placed limits on each plant, forcing it to run at eighty percent capacity. The association also resold ice bought from each plant on the open market for a fixed price, then distributed the profits based on tonnage each plant owner put into the kitty. In a court of law, this "bright idea" is called restraint of trade. The federal government caught wind of the operation; there were charges and countercharges against everyone in the business. In 1951, the government settled on the New Orleans Ice Delivery Corporation as the main culprit and forced the president, Mr. Abernathy, to disband his business.

During the early 1950s, in thanks to the widespread wholesale use of ice, the national ice production was very near what it had been during the top years of home deliveries in the 1920s with forty-two million tons annually, the highest peak since 1938. Icemen continued to celebrate their achievements each winter, at the national ice conventions, which attracted icemen from all over the country to extravagant, desirable locations, occasionally even meeting in Cuba before the embargo. Having reached an earlier peak of 6,000 block ice plants across the United States, the industry continued to be a force to be reckoned with. The industry's strong arm, the National Association of Ice Industries which became the National Ice Association, headquartered in

A. Montz Collard Greens.

Washington, D.C., enlisted the help of powerful lobbyists on a national level, boldly attacking attempts by more modern refrigeration methods to dismantle manufactured ice's reigning status as king of refrigeration. Icemen and their associations relentlessly waged campaigns to promote and foster the use of manufactured ice. Regional and state associations, with at least one ice association in every district, championed the cause with paid executive directors, vice presidents and a full staff. The oldest ice association, the Southern Ice Exchange, began networking in 1889. It held the first gathering of a group of professional ice manufacturers in Memphis, Tennessee, in 1894, in December's off-season in the ice business. This regional trade association, still going strong today, provided instructional lectures and entertainment for the icemen and their wives. One year, it hired Miss Georgia to make an appearance at a convention. State politicians also understood the economic value of ice in their region. Governor Price Daniel proclaimed Texas Ice Day on May 2, 1958. Don't let the simple, hand-painted signs announcing "Ice For Sale" fool you: It was a resolute and influential industry.

The block ice era was a wild and woolly ride for "His Majesty, the Iceman" as the industry helped propel America through the hot and hard times of the first half of the twentieth century. History books have let the manufactured ice business down, but while it was going strong its influence was undeniable. Manufactured ice touched people's everyday lives, either directly as a consumer or indirectly through the wide variety of businesses employing ice in some aspect of their production. The following is a sampling of how and where the industry impacted the health, comfort, and convenience of the nation.

INDIVIDUAL

- ◆ The national problem of scurvy, a liver condition caused by a deficiency of Vitamin C, was practically eliminated through the use of block ice, which preserved the vitamin content in fresh foods during transportation and storage.
- ◆ Chicken eggs could be kept fresh with ice all year-round even though the hens produced in three months nearly half the annual egg supply.
- ◆ Sitting at the soda fountain counter leisurely enjoying an iced cold drink in a sweaty glass became a favorite memory for many Americans.
- ◆ Surprisingly, ice sales increased during Prohibition because Eighteenth Amendment sufferers turned to ice cream stores, confectioners and soft drinks—products that used more ice than drinks at nightclubs.
- ◆ Once the drinking establishments re-opened legally, they created a new drink honoring standard equipment of the day: the Ice Pick, a concoction of iced tea and vodka.
- ◆ "Made-to-order weather" was a slogan for ambulances equipped with ice used to cool the emergency ride to the hospital.
- ◆ The "portable air conditioner," a glorified contraption of ice in a milk jug

Seafood Warehouse employee filling bins with crushed ice at Cristina Ice Service.

with vents and a fan, saved office workers at companies such as Sun Oil, DuPont Chemical Plant, American Cyanide, Continental Oil, Tidewater Shipyards, Tulane University and Loyola University. The devices were also popular at the dog tracks in Hollywood, Florida.

- Baseball fans, rock-n-roll concert dancers, state fair rodeo riders, Jazz Fest partiers—participants in every major event required ice for a good time.
- Debutant parties sparkled with fancy ice bowls that looked great and kept the punch iced cold.
- Huge college dormitory "snowball fights" would break out on campuses that splurged to cover their grounds with the finest, or "snow," shavings from the ice plant.
- Ambitious law school students paid for their education working summer jobs at snow cone stands, selling a product made almost entirely out of ice.
- Using one hundred pounds of ice, Judge Henry Hammond, of Augusta, Georgia, kept his prize flower bushes artificially cold to delay their blooms until the peak moment, when he plucked them from the bushes to win the National Camellia Show in 1949.
- Swimmers indulged in the "super-cooled club pool," such as the one at Piedmont Driving Club of Atlanta, Georgia, by lollygagging on the melting blocks of ice. They had to be careful not to dive into the crystal clear blocks.
- The ultimate ice coolness came at block ice sitting contests where the brave and hot-blooded would wiggle and squirm until someone was dubbed the champion.

COMMERCIAL

- Concrete for bridges, airport runways, nuclear power plants, dams and highway construction is made of sand gravel and ice—not water—when the temperature of the mix has to be kept to exact engineering standards.
- Textile mills added ice to the bleaching, dyeing and mercerizing processes to control the chemical reactions and thereby open up the door for new colors and patterns.
- Chemical plants used ice to control reaction times, which enabled them to produce advanced herbicides and pesticides.
- Oil refiners used ice to cool their black gold.
- Shoe polish, silk products, glue, celluloid for photographic films, printing papers, soap, gelatin and metallurgy all required ice in the creation process.
- Tanners kept their dead alligators fresh and supple with crushed ice until they were ready to be skinned.
- Florist businesses bloomed with a means to keep the fragile beauties fresh and available all year round.
- Hospitals used ice for patients and in the operating rooms.
- Morgues were big users of iced air conditioning equipment.
- Railroad companies provided passengers the cool comfort of ice-activated air-conditioning, using expensive equipment that cost $3,500 per unit.
- Large companies with large payrolls, such as Celotex with 6,000 employees making pressed board from Louisiana sugar cane, and Wilson Cypress Company, in St. Johns River, Florida, helped their employees beat the heat with daily ice deliveries for water coolers.
- The Georgia State Sanatorium, the largest insane asylum in the South in 1907, added a new, larger ice plant to handle the demand for ice in drinks and food preservation.
- Chocolate confectioneries opened in the South once they had ice to keep their candy from melting.
- Sugar mills employed ice to keep bugs at bay.
- Dairy farms needed so much ice they often built their own block plant to cool milk.

- Bakeries used ice to keep rising yeast on track.
- Tea companies consistently passed the taste test using ice to keep their product fresh.
- Tropical Park Stable, in Miami, Florida, bought 1,500 pounds of ice a day for racetrack horses to sooth their aching limbs by standing in rubber tubs filled with ice.
- The booming seafood industry in Bayou La Batre, Alabama, demanded over 500 tons of block ice and 500 tons of fragmentary ice per day, more than was made in the rest of the entire state.
- Fish markets put their goods on beds of crushed ice to keep seafood from spoiling rapidly.
- Poultry plants dropped ice onto defeathered chickens to quickly reduce the temperature of the meat once it was removed from a boiling vat of water.
- Swift Foods produced a national ad campaign in 1950 that proudly announced chicken meat, packed in ice, would be available throughout the year at local grocery stores.
- Grocery stores placed produce on a packed layer of ice to keep fruits and vegetables cool and moist.
- The Santa Fe Railroad used so much ice in 1910 it built a plant with a per-day capacity of 225 tons to chill daily carloads of fruit.
- Five million pounds of ice were used each day for Rio Grand Valley produce in Texas.
- If an early frost claimed the peach crop or summer heat withered the peas, ice sales would melt as well.
- Ninety-eight percent of all perishables, beans, tomatoes, watermelons, sweet corn, cabbage, lettuce, celery, spinach, broccoli, mustard and collard greens, little English peas, peaches, grapes, apples, oranges, grapefruit, and many more, were shipped under ice during the 1950s.
- When the world's biggest produce market, the State Farmers Market in Atlanta Georgia, opened in 1960, it knew it would need so much ice that an ice distribution center opened right alongside it.

GOVERNMENT

- "Death to destructive insects," proclaimed the Government Food Laboratories (precursor to Food And Drug Administration) upon their new discoveries of the power of ice.
- "Ice produces a state much like that of the sleeping snake in winter or the hibernation of a bear until spring," explained the authorities.
- The public had to be enlightened to the fact that nearly rotten food would not be revived in the icebox.
- Experts debated the question of preservation of eggs—were they edible after three, six, or twelve months? The modern health department says the answer is one month.
- Scientists tried pushing the boundaries of the uses for ice. Could they freeze milk? (No, it didn't taste so good later on.)
- Government specialists ate twenty-seven month-old fish preserved in cold storage with a coating of ice, renewed every few months, declaring there was virtually no deterioration and but little loss in palatability.
- Whenever military bases ran maneuvers in the summertime, the sergeants were sure to keep the recruits cool with ice in their canteens.
- During World War I, one of the busiest military ice plants produced 500 tons of ice per day.
- Munitions factories used ice to maintain strict control of temperature and humidity, and Allied ships kept their explosives cool with ice in the hull.
- Military contracts spiked at chemical plants during the entanglement of the Vietnam War, which in turn made chemical plants demand more ice to cool chemical reactions.

THE MELT DOWN

During my childhood in the 1960s, my paternal grandmother's kitchen no longer had the old iceboxes she'd used for so many decades. They had been replaced by several deep freezers and a couple of electric refrigerators. She had long since gotten over the effort the old iceboxes required, preferring the "less messy,

less high maintenance" electrical refrigerators of the day. Far from what we would term user-friendly, these early refrigerators still had to be defrosted periodically. One had to be careful not to get impatient and attack the thick build-up of frost with an ice pick, inevitably puncturing the sealed casing of Freon as the hiss of escaping gas instantly ended the life of the freezer and refrigerator. However, Bigmama still did not have one ice tray anywhere in her house. Instead, her husband and son brought her bags of chopped, crystal clear oblongs of block ice. At my mother's house, we used the foggy cubes made in the home freezer, but at Bigmama's house no one ever dreamed of using ice of such ill repute. When the whole family gathered for Sunday dinners, the older, more dexterous cousins used the ice pick to break up the ice when it was too big to fit in dainty crystal glasses filled with freshly-brewed sweetened tea, garnished with a fresh sprig of mint plucked from the backyard. The ice at Bigmama's house was smoother in my mouth, easier to bite and make loud crunching noises—but never at the dinner table. Mealtime was a serious affair, but during the rest of the time, we had free-reign of the opulent house and grounds built with ice money, often playing King of the Hill in the short front yard that abruptly ended at the concrete sidewalk down below. I also remember playing kickball in the parking lot of the church a few blocks away, staying out too late after dinner on summer evenings. The euphonious songs of crickets and frogs told me I was about to get in trouble once again.

I never experienced the fun of running behind the ice truck, but there was a mosquito truck with a fog machine all the neighborhood children chased, apparently not absorbing too much DDT to affect us. My immediate family had a milkman who delivered milk to our refrigerator, not to the door. He came in the back door, always unlocked, checked the fridge for what we had, knew how much three rambunctious girls and a tennis-playing mom consumed in a week, and left us our supply. He also left us ice cream, the amount depending on how much I could con him (and my mother) into for the week. At Christmas, he had ice cream Christmas trees on a stick, covered in red and green sprinkles, that were better than any ice cream treat I've ever had since. His was one of the last remaining home delivery routes in the city, with the dismantling of such a tradition many years in the making.

The very beginning of the end of the icebox and home ice delivery came when a French Cistercian monk and physics teacher, Marcel Audiffren, demonstrated to a fascinated gathering in Paris his invention of an electrically driven sealed-container refrigerator that used sulfur dioxide gas. This self-regulating machine, for which he received patents in a number of countries in 1895, was the precursor to the first home mechanical refrigerator. For the next thirty years, the big hold-ups for practical use of his invention were the invention of miniature compressors and stable gases. After World War I, the country was experiencing a boom in the automobile industry. General Motors, one of the dominating companies of the day, put its backing into Frigidaire, a company pursuing a reasonable functioning household refrigerator. Together, they discovered synthetic refrigerants called halocarbons, better known as CFCs.

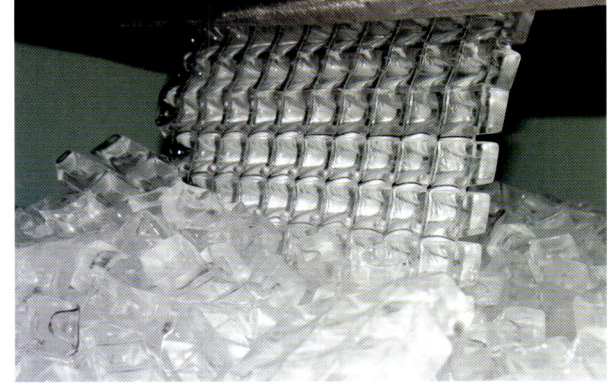

With the inventions of the electric motor, sealed system, automatic controls and the new nonflammable, (theoretically) nontoxic refrigerant, the household electrical refrigerator was on an unstoppable march to take over the icebox. The block plants put up a great fight. They focused on the superior benefits of their product, and they joined forces to begin advertising, something heretofore not needed nor valued. It was a valiant but fatal fight. In

1926, 2,000 mechanical refrigerators were sold. By 1931, one million models were sold, and in 1937, nearly three million were sold. Widespread use of the icebox lasted through the 1940s, but the ease of the electric refrigerator triumphed. By 1950, the vast majority of wealthy and middle-income city dwellers used a mechanical refrigerator. Regardless of the trouble of the traditional iceboxes with the block in the back and a drip pan at the bottom, many people were unwilling to completely give up something they so loved for its ability to keep produce crisp and fresh. They simply moved their iceboxes out to the garage where they kept their produce or used it as a spare box. Conversely, the heavily rural population of the South was generally too poor to get new refrigerators. This economic constraint contributed significantly to the eleven million families who had ice refrigerators in 1950. Those who were still relying on iceboxes in the 1960s most likely wished they had mechanical boxes, but they simply could not afford them.

Another inventor, Willis Carrier, was busy at the turn of the 20th century working on inventions designed to cool industrial machines. He received U.S. Patent #808897 in 1906 for his "Apparatus for Treating Air." His greatest achievement came less than twenty years later when, in 1921, he designed a safer and more efficient method for air conditioning large spaces. With this "centrifugal chiller" breakthrough, the idea of cooling a room for human comfort took off, changing the pattern and movements of humanity forever.

Fifty years later, people like my maternal grandmother were still saving the air conditioning for Sunday company, but businesses that had relied on ice to cool public spaces, like movie theaters and large offices, switched to mechanical air conditioning equipment when the price came down, slowly eating away at some of the commercial ice accounts of the day.

The next inroads for artificial coolness came from a bet on a golf course in Minneapolis, Minnesota. Fredrick Jones, in 1937, told his boss he had an idea for mounting an air conditioner in the forehead cargo area of a truck. No one believed him because the trucks were too bouncy to have any type of air conditioning system in them so the idea went no further. One year later, Mr. Jones' boss, Mr. Joseph Numero, made a bet on the golf course against one of his business comrades that Mr. Jones could create an air-conditioning device that would function in a truck. Mr. Jones came through on the bet, inventing automobile refrigeration for long-haul trucks, which in turn earned him a place in the almanac of famous African-American inventors. The two men formed Numero and Jones Company, in Minneapolis, to begin making compact, automatic, shockproof air conditioning for truck transportation of foods. Despite the fact that block ice not only cooled produce, but provided essential moisture, this new refrigeration system was preferred because truck drivers no longer had to stop every few hours to replenish the ice supply. As the interstates replaced the highway routes, truckers found it more difficult to have easy access to the old block ice plants built in the center of towns and along railroad tracks, further adding to the demise of ice as a refrigerant for overland produce transportation.

Railroads, having used block ice to cool their cargo since J.B. Sutherland of Detroit, Michigan, patented the iced refrigerated railroad car in 1867, slowly adapted Jones' new mechanical refrigeration system for their cargo and passenger cars. This was an added blow to the already dwindling need for ice on the new, faster produce trains that required less block ice per route. The produce industry, previously part of the backbone of rail and block ice businesses, was going through a major transition itself. The 1950s and 1960s brought a dramatic increase in the amount of food shipped in frozen format. Frozen food takes up less space, uses fewer rail cars and requires less ice than fresh foods. To make matters worse, railroads were losing much of their produce business to the trucking industry. Truck routes were far more flexible and trucks had direct access to wholesale food distributors and stores. This was good news for the overland hauling business, which was committed to mechanical refrigeration, but more bad news for the block ice business. The new air conditioning systems also found their way into shrimp and seafood boats, allowing fishermen to fish until their hearts' content, no longer dependent on when the ice ran out. The new systems, with consistent cold temperatures, didn't leave any hot pockets in the hull like blown ice did.

The utilities industry was undergoing its own metamorphosis that consequently had a negative affect on block ice plants. As more and more homes started using electricity or natural gas for their sole source of heat, ice factories lost their regular wintertime income from the sale of coal. Compounding the problem, when the coal quit coming to town, the railroad company quit using those local lines altogether, so the remaining ice transportation business dried up with the end of the coal business. Local ice factories continued to operate on a limited basis for strictly local customers, but the loss of both the wintertime income and the summer sales of ice to the railroads eventually took its toll on small town plants.

Prior to World War II, ice had been considered a manufacturing product. To procure the necessary materials for the much needed ice production in the war effort, the Food and Drug Administration decided to categorize ice as a food product. After the war, the label still remained, bringing with that classification strict sanitation laws. New inspections, rules and regulations forced plants to spend a great deal of money to conform if they wanted to continue selling bagged or block ice for human consumption. No hands could touch the ice. A 300-pound block could not sit out in the open air on a dock. The block could no longer be dragged across the dock by an employee and his pair of tongs, but now had to be kept behind closed doors in the storage room. Plants had to have special permits to bag ice. Code dates had to be stamped on bags in some states where the vendor was required to remove the ice if it went out of date. Yet another added expense from the food label was the need for plants to carry product liability insurance to protect themselves should something go awry. Ultimately, this cost of cooperation put some plants out of business.

Grocery stores, once displaying produce on lovely piles of crushed ice, switched to the misting and drenching system for coolness and humidity. Catfish farms, the new lease on life for Delta ice plants, found a new way of injecting oxygen straight into the transportation vats. Vending machines, sitting outside on a sidewalk or by the elevator in a hallway, provide chilled liquid refreshment without a piece of ice in sight. The invention of the Styrofoam ice chest in the 1960s was a new marvel, since the entire chest could be transported for outings and other events. Styrofoam, employing trapped air as insulation, required less ice to keep cold drinks cold than non-insulated carriers. Water kegs with large chunks of floating block ice were replaced by electric water coolers, not as cold, not as refreshing some might say, but with far less effort.

Despite all these encroachments, the block ice business was still going strong during the early 1950s, prospering from the many commercial accounts running hard and heavy with the use of block ice. This industrial need for block ice was more prominent in larger cities where the hustle and bustle of enterprise was taking place. Not all small-town ice plants were able to adapt from home delivery to the new cultural and technological uses of block ice. For a city plant, however, there was so much commercial need for ice, it could move from one area of concentration into a new market without too much trouble. Big plants felt very secure in their futures, even in the middle of the 1950s. They did not foresee that the real competition, the biggest, baddest culprit of them all, would come from within the ranks of the ice world itself, eventually making the block ice world obsolete.

Right after World War II, as the block ice industry was gearing up for more business with surplus military equipment, newcomers to the ice business were rethinking the entire process of how to make ice. "Why," these newcomers asked, "make block ice only to turn around and crush the ice into smaller forms? Why not make it small to begin with?" It was a reasonable line of thought, considering how much ice was chipped and crushed versus how little went

"Jamie" bagging fragmentary ice, Bay Ice Company.

1934 Bruce McBeth natural gas engine with broken crank shaft, MICO.

out in block form. They were willing to invest in a new technology for chipped ice production that had been waiting out in the wings, eager to have its chance at center stage.

Although the "tube ice machine" was invented by Vogt Ice in 1937, the technology didn't really take off until the 1950s, gaining its stride as the Age of Aquarius descended on America. These "fragmentary" ice machines so satisfied the needs of the modern market, they revolutionized the commercial ice-making industry. The tube ice machine produces ice in a tube and then cuts it into short cylinders in ready-to-package size. The machines are small, physically taking up little floor space compared to the immense equipment used in ammonia block ice plants. They operate with very little labor involved and can produce ice around the clock with little or no supervision. Fragmentary machines operate on fewer kilowatts of electricity than block plants. These new ice machines didn't need engineers, can pullers, or dockworkers nor did they require a big building with elaborate floor plans and multiple tiers of floors. An automated bag device could be attached to the fragmentary machine, which eliminated the need to have anyone stand at the chipper, bag in hand, as the block was slowly crushed. In 1961, the entire machine cost from $1,800 to $15,000, nowhere near the $25,000 capital invested just for an ice plant expansion twenty-five years earlier (without accounting for inflation). Everything about the block ice plant was being thrown out the window, leaving the owners scrambling for their survival.

Mostly, the block ice industry fought this competition any way it could, even forbidding any block ice plant from joining the National Ice Association if it installed an automatic icemaker. The technology was too irresistible, though. The machines were so efficient, some block plants found it more economical to buy bagged ice from one of the new fragmentary plants, pay for the shipping and sell it at their own plants, saving the block ice for other purposes.

Kenny Cristina, co-owner Cristina Ice Service, standing on a Vogt P-24 tube ice machine.

Not only were block ice plants competing against other ice plants making fragmentary ice, they discovered many customers no longer needed ice plants of either type. The fragmentary machines were so self-contained, they could be installed anywhere there was water and electricity. Anyone could make ice with an "on-premise" ice machine. The machines could be any size—small enough to produce only 200 pounds a day for restaurants and hotels, or up to twenty tons a day for a poultry plant. The machine could be installed in an office break-room, a county fair drink line or tucked away right underneath the sink at a bar. Ice became available anytime, day or night, when and where it was needed. In 1961, in St. Petersburg, Florida, fragmentary ice machines made seventy-five percent of the ice used throughout the entire city—by individuals purchasing fragmentary ice produced at local ice plants for grocery stores and gas stations and by commercial businesses making their own ice at their own companies.

There is an adage in the ice business that there are never three cool summers in a row. A note of optimism for those having a hard time, it could not withstand the onslaught of the on-premise ice machines. Block ice, inch for inch, has less surface area than modern fragmentary ice so it melts ever-so-slowly. Old-timers would curse you if you suggested they get ice from "Clarks," traders who sold fast-melting fragmentary ice. However, the rest of the commercial world took to the automated machines like kids to banana popsicles. In 1961, the national total of fragmentary ice machines produced one and a half times more ice than the "real" ice industry was making—thirty-three million tons versus twenty-two million tons.

Plants trying to transition from block ice to fragmentary ice were hit-or-miss. The old plants were too antiquated for the new machinery. For most plants, there was nothing left to do but to shut down. Many families turned off the lights and flipped over their shingle for the last time without the chance

to sell any equipment or the business, much less the land located in what had often become an undesirable section of town. Eventually, there were so few block plants and so many automatic machines that the National Ice Association relinquished its stand against the fragmentary machines and admitted manufacturers making ice by any means. The new ice-manufacturing companies understood the trends and desires of the modern American business world and they introduced a new era that both brought down the old ice regime and moved manufactured ice into a new viable market. As natural ice had been replaced by manufactured block ice, so block ice was replaced by fragmentary ice. Today, fragmentary ice is a thriving industry in its own right with one national ice corporation capable of producing 17,000 tons of fragmentary ice daily.

A few block plants had niches to keep them going, but even they ran into trouble trying to transition from simple times when the ice business had been predominantly a local one. The control of money, now concentrated in corporations operating in a national and global economy, clashed with the good-ole-boy handshake in style, service, scale, time and availability that lasted far past its usefulness. If the sons were running the family business, many kept the same practices of their fathers, whose antiquated know-how and savvy did not translate into the new era. Many of the old-timers never increased their prices to reflect economic inflation. Everything seemed hopeless in the block ice world.

On top of that, so many icemen were dying. Managers were dying, leaving no one there to operate the plant with any depth of knowledge and integrity. Owners were dying, leaving no one to oversee the business or, their wills could be tied up in probate court for so many years that the businesses suffered greatly. Obituaries were the front page news of every issue of the trade journals from the early 1960s through the 1970s. The rest of the pages reflected atypical attitudes that had invaded the industry—impatience, fear and suspicion—with every columnist complaining nonstop about the sorry demeanor at the ice conventions. They complained that no one was there anymore, leaving the few attendees wondering if the missing were dead or if just the businesses were dead and gone. Losing their own advertising customers weekly, the trade journals' scant pages reflected the appalling condition of the once-mighty industry when ice was king.

Block ice, once a luxury, then a necessity, was no longer even needed by most of its former customers. The exodus from block ice manufacturing business that began in the 1960s continued unabated for the next twenty-five years. It's a depressing end to a wonderful era in American culture. Not all is lost, however, as there are still a few plants scattered across the nation producing block ice with the old-fashioned machinery.

Remains of concrete foundations used to keep engines and compressors from vibrating across the floor, Farmer's Ice Company, Crystal Springs, Miss.

FROZEN ASSETS

The year I spent living at the Morris Ice Company had been stimulatingly adventurous as I began to fall in love with everything I saw and learned about the old block ice era. I began to feel a necessity to care for all of it, the architecture and equipment practically begging me to provide for its future.

Because our company never folded as a business but just stopped making ice, the fate of the old plant and its adjoining property is still on the table at the annual family-filled board of directors meetings. Most of that group is of a practical nature whereas I secretly held sublime ambitions for our historical corner of the block ice world.

The more information I learned about the business, the more I wanted to turn our plant into a museum honoring the impact block ice had on the Deep South. It was ripe with artifacts and memorabilia from the block ice era saved by my uncle, grandfather and great grandfather. The amazing 1930s upstairs office, complete with yellowing papers from that time, was so intact it looked like a made-up Hollywood movie scene. The downstairs thirty-foot-long ice storage room added on after the plant's original construction would make a perfect new home for the photographs, journals, magazines and bookkeeping records currently scattered throughout the plant. We still had so much of the original equipment used to make ice, the engines, compressors, generators, fly wheels and the electric switchboard, that visitors could easily

ponder how much work it had been to make a 300-pound cake of ice. The platform, of course, was covered so patrons would have a protected spot to enter the ice museum even during the notorious summer thunderstorms that drop two inches of water in an hour, every single afternoon for three months running. Until word of mouth spread on the wonders of the block ice era, some of the one-story ice-handling rooms could be used by local artists, turning the tiny doors used for sliding ice out onto the dock into light-giving windows.

As for my future home, I envisioned the nation's most amazing downtown living space from the forty-foot by forty-foot by forty-foot old ice storage room; a perfect cube meets a perfect vision. The room's cypress walls, lined with ammonia coils up top, are soundproof with three feet of brick and an insulating layer of air. I could play the drums. I could build large metal sculptures. I could create a big platform out of multi-leveled monkey bars for an open bedroom. And, most importantly, I could live free of conventional walls that create chopped-up tiny rooms. This cool, urban cube would remain a cube, not become a replica of a suburban apartment relocated into an urban space with the catchy but false name of "loft."

The imagined door on the ground level would lead outside to what would become a New Orleans-style secret garden, its eastern border defined by the abandoned twenty-five-foot-long water pump. I intended to remove one side of the pump to expose the interior pipes, which I would transform into an extreme industrial water feature. Two other sides of the garden would be formed by the original exterior brick walls of the plant that come together at right angles, thus creating an exotic forty-foot-tall hide-a-way. The final side would be a wall of existing vegetation—plus a wire fence camouflaged in the foliage for security. Back inside the cube, an adjacent wall would have a door cut in it, at about a second-floor level, which would lead out to an imagined screen porch resting over the existing roof of the garage. About thirty feet high on the next wall over, I imagined putting up huge, and I mean huge, windows to let in all the southern light, filling the cube with bright sunshine but not direct rays. The windows would open up onto the roof of the long ice-creating tank room, leading to a field day of possibilities for an urban junkie like myself. The fourth wall still had the old indoor elevator, previously used to stack ice during the winter months of inventory build-up. I would use it to take my friends and me through the existing hatch that opens onto the roof of the storage room itself.

(opposite) Raymond "Yank" Harris, employee of Cristina Ice Service;
(above) Antiques and Junk Store, located at former Crystal Ice and Fuel Company.

Under the shade of the enormous backyard hackberry tree and surrounded by a three-foot-high brick wall that would keep everyone safe from vertigo, I was going to build the coveted roof garden I'd dreamed of having since I first saw one in some New York magazine. My skyline view, though, looked out over the parking lot and railroad tracks to a vista of the modest downtown buildings of Jackson, Mississippi. Looking back the other direction, the view was nothing but treetops and a rural country landscape where the police department boards its horses that roam out in grassy fields created by flood plains of the Pearl River.

The manifestation of this dream got as far as one onsite consultation with a homebuilder, an e-mail to the home makeover network, a letter to an architect friend, and one cool outdoor shower I built in the back of the lot. A ten-foot-long metal sign announcing "Truck Icing, Morris Ice Company" became one of the shower-stall walls. No hot water and insistent, biting flies and mosquitoes kept the shower from becoming a popular replacement for the one at the distant country club. Ultimately, I suspected my vagabond soul would become restless after waking up in the same spot too many years in a row, regardless of my ability to woo the Board with the prodigiousness of my plans.

A couple of years later, when I was following the trail of abandoned ice plants to document the block ice era, I was thrilled to find numerous, more determined, perhaps less nostalgic, individuals who had either successfully kept their ice plants alive or converted a closed plant into a new enterprise with a vitality of its own.

TOWNHOUSES AND NIGHT CLUBS

Snuggled in the heart of the Blues country in the Mississippi Delta is a small old block ice plant that took on a new life in 1966 as the first townhouse in Clarksdale. Ten years before, the block ice plant had supported the adjacent Garmon Ice Cream Company and Ice Plant, the most popular ice cream parlor in town with sixteen carhops for the drive-in, not drive-through, service. After the business shut down, Tommy Garmon and his wife, Virginia, still owned the building so they decided to do something with the family property. Virginia Garmon, an artist originally from New Orleans, perused old mansions and salvage yards for mantles, fireplaces, trim molding, bathtubs and anything else she could find to turn the defunct business into a home where she and her husband could raise their family. She incorporated tiles from the soda fountain counters of the ice creamery into the motif of the living room. The ceiling fan used to blow flies away from customers is in the den. The old block ice part of the building is a wonderful two-story atrium, now tended by the new owner, Nashville, Tennessee musician Tommy Polk. His passion and historical inclinations have forestalled the demolition of yet one more old block ice plant.

Many years before hearing about the refurbished ice plant in McComb, Mississippi, the hot nightclub called The Ice House, I had a nice evening at another ice plant-turned-bar along the Mississippi River. When I inquired about the Delta establishment during my month-long trip across Mississippi, no one seemed to know anything about it. It is possible that I was simply in an old warehouse-turned-bar and my imagination merged the warehouse with the possibility of an ice plant, my family ice plant, having the same fate. While my grandmother was still alive, there was little chance the Morris Ice Company would ever have become a successful evening establishment;

Interior of Tommy Polk residence, former Garmon Ice Cream Company and Ice Plant; Mr. Polk at home; Rear view of former Garmon Ice Cream Company and Ice Plant.

Front entrance, The Ice House, McComb, Miss.

she hardly tolerated a couple of beers, "nasty olds" as she called them, in her refrigerator for a few hours. This lucid memory made me anxious to lay my eyes on the McComb plant, to verify its existence both as an operating nightclub and as an old icehouse. When my boyfriend and I drove up to the plant to check it out, we had a sinking sensation. The place looked abandoned. Fortunately, we figured out that we'd simply arrived too early in the day for anything to be going on yet. We were equally satisfied that the building had indeed been a block ice plant, as it wears its history on its sleeve. The old go-get-em spirit of the place must permeate the structure as it survived two partial fires and one effort at demolition in 1977. The old block ice plant now houses several bar areas, conference spaces and a restaurant. Trees growing in the rear storage area make up the luscious outdoor seating area called "Yesterday's Patio." At the entrance to the complex, a National Register of Historic Places plaque gives a brief history of the building. Big, old black-and-white photographs hang in one of the smaller bars for the curious patron to discover what block ice was and how it was made.

MUSEUMS AND ANTIQUE STORES

Always happy to find any part of a block ice plant still standing regardless of its current use, I was really thrilled to find out about the laborious efforts of a couple of cousins in LaPlace, Louisiana, who wanted to turn their grandfather's highly successful business into a public museum. A. Montz Packaging Company started out as one man, Armand Montz, Sr., his very healthy green thumb, and the resultant vegetables in need of ice for their trip up North. While his green thumb proved to be very productive, the rest of his fingers must've been golden because the Montz operation not only had its own block ice plant by 1914, the plant supplied water for the surrounding town of LaPlace until 1969. The plant produced its own electricity, with enough leftover to sell spare kilowatts in a twenty-five-mile radius, until Mr. Montz sold the electrical rights to Louisiana Power & Light in 1927. Mr. Monz developed his own frozen foods operation with his own label, A. Montz Frozen Foods, in 1939. The vegetable-packing plant was not only the first Southern plant to process and ship frozen foods, but it grew so much so fast that the business caught the attention of food giant Birds Eye. The corporation wanted to buy Mr. Montz' business if it could use its own label. That didn't sound like any kind of deal for this successful entrepreneur, who went on to ship under his own label until 1962. Before Mr. Montz got out of the business altogether, he owned more than 600 acres for produce production and still needed to buy from local growers to satisfy the demand for A. Montz frozen vegetables. During World War II, Mr. Montz put thirty German POWs to work in the ice and packing plants and another thirty general laborers in the fields. The prisoners found the working conditions so amiable one wrote Mr. Montz a letter once he got back to Germany, requesting that the owner pay his way back to the United States so he could come back to work for him, an offer the American declined. Mr. Montz, as always, was savvy not to take on any additional laborers, believing the produce production boom was not going to last much longer. New heavy industry was coming into the Mississippi River area and even large-scale farming operations could not compete with the higher wages and the easier workload. Mr. Montz phased out the processing plant from 1958 to 1962, although his children, Nem Montz, Armand Montz, Jr. and Alice Mae Montz Maurin operated the block ice business for another sixteen years.

The following generation, grandsons Gerard Montz and his cousin, Gilbert Maurin, entered the business after a fire struck the main icehouse in 1989. For three years, they gathered and sorted memorabilia. They began tackling the multitude of run-down old buildings, the maintenance and blacksmith shop, the warehouse, the seed house, the power plant, the kitchen, and the equipment storage building with hopes of starting a museum. Hurricane Andrew, causing over $25 billion worth of damage across south Florida and Louisiana in 1992, spun off a tornado that took down all but two of the original buildings on the Montz property. Mr. Maurin passed away in 2001, but Mr. Montz remains unfettered in his efforts to share the history of his grandfather's business. He put together a small museum in one of the remaining support buildings. He organized an educational display at the local St. John the Baptist Parish Library. Rightly so, Mr. Montz feels there is too much history with his

Photo courtesy Gerard Montz.

grandfather's business and the block ice era just to let it disappear into oblivion. His efforts have paid off. The state of Louisiana has honored the many contributions of the A. Montz Packaging and ice business with a roadside historical marker.

In the small remote Delta town of Friar's Point, Mississippi, the local ice plant had been home to a fellow ice plant resident, Mrs. Katherine Arenz. Mrs. Arenz grew up a couple of hours away in the small community of Blue Mountain. In the 1920s, that town had neither ice delivery nor coal delivery. She says she remembers hearing about ice, but has no early memories of ever using it. Instead of using coal for heat, she remembers her family cutting down trees for fuel. After getting her teaching certificate in 1934, Mrs. Arenz moved to the Friar's Point area in the Delta. She could make more money as a teacher there than anywhere else in the state, staying at a teacher's home with room and board for $22.50 a month. A couple of years later, she married Buck Arenz and moved into his apartment in back of the Crystal Ice and Fuel Company. Her new husband had been living there for ten years as the ice factory manager, a common arrangement in ice plants that ran twenty-four hours a day. Upon the arrival of his wife, the single, small back room was expanded into a couple of rooms. Like many people in quiet Southern towns, she fondly remembers being rocked to sleep with the distinctive chug-chug-chug of the one-stroke diesel engines running all night long to make ice. More than fifty years later, Mrs. Arenz recalls her life at the ice plant saying, "We were young. We didn't care. We had all we needed."

The ice plant closed its doors when coal trains quit coming to town in the 1950s and sat vacant until it was purchased as an antiques repair shop. Once the new owner fixed the leaks and cleaned it out some, the antiques went on display in the showroom, sitting side-by-side with the old engines the plant used to make ice. The antique restoration business has faded into an antiques and junk shop, but at least the building still stands and the doors to the old block ice plant are open on Saturdays and Sundays. Ironically, the old "Ice For Sale" sign itself is now up for sale as memorabilia for the folk art enthusiast. The engines were sold and put to use at a nearby cotton gin, their single stroke pistons still clacking away and still rocking the ground underfoot.

TRADITIONAL USES

Pascagoula Ice and Freezer Company, the first functioning ice plant I found still making 300-pound blocks of ice the old-fashioned way, doesn't rely on the block ice business for its survival. That part of the operation keeps running as homage to the father of the three brothers running the plant, Mr. Quin Gautier, honored by the International Packaged Ice Association as the 1965 Hall of Fame recipient. The main business is processing and flash-freezing shrimp for national and international exportation, but local customers come up everyday to get block ice. One of their regular customers is Bozo's Grocery, the fabulous third-generation seafood market and delicious lunch spot. It sells only local seafood, kept cold on a bed of crushed block ice. The to-die-for Gulf Coast shrimp po-boys are becoming more and more of a divine treat since eighty percent of all shrimp consumed in America is imported, most of which comes from farm-raised ponds. For now, it's nice to know that independently-owned businesses are prospering in such a mutual relationship.

In Savannah, Georgia, Triangle Ice Company, another block ice business whose early days relied heavily on the seafood industry, now has a very modern packaged-ice business with a limited production of block ice, but it's made using very modern equipment. The plant, built in 1904, used a large system pulling sixteen 300-pound cans at a time. The operation was so large the blocks were carried across the road via a conveyor belt. The belt ran through a covered bridge for use in the seafood blast-freezer business until 1968 or so. Fire and repeated vandalism forced the owners to tear down the large tank room sometime in the 1970s, but the rest of the massive, old structure, four stories of ice storage rooms, awaits renovation into dry storage rooms.

David Gautier, co-owner, Pascagoula Ice and Freezer Company.

Triangle Ice Company, Savannah, Ga.; Clinebell carving block maker, Triangle Ice Company; David Bush, Triangle Ice Company employee.

On the first floor, in a four-foot by fifteen-foot section, is the current block ice business. Due to demand, generally from chefs for banquet events, Triangle Ice Company went back into the block ice business, but now they make ice using two extremely modern upright metal compartments. They make absolutely clear blocks of ice devoid of the typical air stream or feather. The compartments, in the traditional one-foot by two-feet by four-feet shape, are simply freezers. Each container makes one block at a time, removed with a pulley once it's frozen solid. For each new block of ice made the water is poured into a clear plastic bag that lines the container. A blower, located at one end, keeps the water bubbling so it "won't turn on you" by going white, says David Bush, the plant's resident ice expert of forty-eight years. During his career, Bush has pulled ice, loaded it, hauled it and stood in the freezer room bagging ice by hand into seven-pound bags, one at a time. Now he oversees the automated section of the bagging area, making sure the machines do his old job. The veteran employee has transitioned from ancient to modern technology in every aspect of the business, from using tongs to drag the bare blocks across the dock to overseeing machinery that individually shrink-wraps each block as it comes out of the freezing machine, filling up the storage room with ice encased in plastic.

Not all modern ice comes out crystal clear. Metropolitan New Orleans, party central for any occasion, has two block ice plants, both owned by the Cristina family, which produce ice for any occasion in town. Pastel colors are added to the water, creating pink and blue blocks for Easter parades. Purple and gold and green blocks come out of the cans for Mardi Gras parties. Sometimes, the blocks come out with jeans frozen inside for a tabletop shoot for a sleek magazine advertisement. Or, a block comes out of the tank with a can of soda inside it for a Swedish marketing campaign. For that particular event, the block of ice containing the drink, instead of the other way around,

Old-fashioned 300-pound block ice on platform;
New block ice, wrapped in plastic.

was trucked down to the French Quarter for its exotic background ambience. There, in the middle of the street, a scantily clad model using a chain saw with pure determination was retrieving her favorite soda no matter how much effort it took. Another time at one of the Cristina ice plants, a New York ad agency showed up with a full entourage to shoot an album cover for an up-and-coming rap star. They created a cave out of existing blocks in the freezing cold storage room. They distorted the scene with colored, hot lights everywhere. They made a big throne for the rapper and a bevy of half-naked girls surrounded their royal king and *voila*! Nothing. Apparently the scene didn't work because that cover layout never hit the streets. But, for the fourth generation cousins David Romig and Kenny Cristina running the plant, the result was the same: cold, hard cash coming in to keep the family business going.

The cousins have their own slew of memories of growing up at their family's ice plants. Every little nook and cranny can trigger something from the past, even the ditches that were a big challenge to jump across when the men were small boys. Back then, the Cristina family had many ice plants scattered around southern Louisiana. The flagship plant, Cristina Ice and Cold Storage, located about fifteen miles west of New Orleans in Kenner, has been in the family since in 1907. Built by the Cristina, Scheneckenberger and Watney families, it supplied ice to chill produce from surrounding farms in transport down to the French Market, a day's journey away by horse and buggy on dirt roads alongside the Mississippi River levees. In Gretna, Louisiana, across the Mississippi River from the city, another one of their ice plants sat alongside the LaFourche District Levee on Front Street. In 1952, the fickle and corrupt Levee Board decided the ice plant, with a tank that was riveted together, not welded, was in the way of the levee and forced them to relocate. Mr. Robert Cristina, who was in charge of the ice plant at the time, quickly secured some questionable property, much to the chagrin of the rest of the family. Within weeks, he found a survey crew on the corner of the new property marking out lines for the superhighway coming curbside of his new ice plant. At first distraught, he quickly changed his construction plans and repositioned the ice plant toward the rear of the lot in order to leave room for a gas and convenience store out front. Just about anything located right off the Westbank Expressway does well so the extra revenue from the pumps and provisions kept the ice business prosperous long past the time other plants had shut their doors. Today, the property is in the thick of suburban

Louis Robertson, Jr., third-generation employee, and David Romig,
fourth-generation owner, Cristina Ice Service.

sprawl and the gas business, the convenience store and the ice plant are gone, but the family has an extremely lucrative rental agreement with one of the oldest, biggest, and best-tasting French fries and hamburger joints in the world—McDonald's.

It's been said that the ice business is a good one hundred days—from Memorial Day in May until Labor Day in September. But even in the hot, notoriously humid climate of the bayou state, with a longer summer season than most, the slow winter months make it hard to keep the block business prosperous. The Cristina family now has only two locations left, one in Marrero, about ten miles south of New Orleans and the original one in Kenner. Since the 1980s when the great grandsons Romig and Cristina took over daily operations, the duo has sold ice to produce markets, the seafood industry, industrial businesses and walk-up customers. The only way the two men keep their remaining two plants and one vendor icebox operational is by adaptability, creativity, love and sacrifice—by acting as their own mechanic, electrical engineer and ammonia engineer; by having employees with a lineage as long in the ice business as their own; by missing out on every summer for the past thirty-two years due to work; and by never having a Fourth of July off.

In Cairo, Georgia, just north of Tallahassee, Florida, David Hildebrandt, owner of M&M Ice and Cold Storage Company, isn't a fourth, third or anything generation iceman. He went out of his way to enter the "dying" ice business in 2000, switching from refrigeration engineer by trade to the new owner of a 1940s block ice plant so he could live closer to his family. The bread and butter of M&M Ice and Cold Storage for the last sixty-five years has been selling ice to chill shipments of sweet, tender, temperamental Georgia corn. If it is chilled in a typical railroad refrigeration car or semi-tractor truck using mechanical refrigeration, the corn kernels get hard, making the corn unsalable. Corn needs cold temperatures, and it needs the moisture that only melting ice can provide. In fact, the agricultural demand in the region is so great there is another operating block ice plant in the same area, Adel Ice Company. Should that demand not stay true, M&M Ice and Cold Storage is diversifying into an even more demanding arena—perfectly clear block ice for carving. As always, icemen take great pride in producing a clear block of ice, but ice carvers must be the most demanding group, often refusing a block if it isn't to their exact specifications. Personally inspecting the blocks throughout

Trucker loading 42,200 pounds of ice into eighteen-wheeler, M&M Ice and Cold Storage; Tank room, M&M Ice and Cold Storage.

the freezing process, Mr. Hildebrandt uses mostly traditional equipment in his labor-intensive, back-breaking method of drop-tube and needle-air-hose that leaves the tiniest air feather, if one at all. The long-standing association of ice and a good time remains true for his new crowd found on numerous Miami cruise ships. They cater to the travel-hungry Americans who adore the carved centerpieces on fancy buffet tables.

The art of ice carving is centuries old, dating back to early times in Chinese history, when only natural harvested ice was available. Although I found little evidence of ice carving during the early part of the twentieth century, it is very much alive and well today and is clearly not limited to use at banquets and on cruise ships. You'll find it's not limited at all, if you check the diverse sculptures people create at the many ice-carving festivals, competitions and winter celebrations held any time of the year around the globe. Most of the festivals are up in northern climates so the art can have a longer display life, but there are plenty of summer concerts and fundraisers that include 300-pound block ice carvings as part of the entertainment. Professional carvers, members of the National Ice Carving Association, pull out their chain saws, drills and chisels to vie for gold, silver and bronze medals from certified judges. They can win their way to the Cultural Olympics held every four years in conjunction with the International Winter Olympics. At the 2004 International Snow and Ice Festival in the city of Antwerp, Belgium, ice carvers put the world of sixteenth century artist Peter Paul Rubens on ice, creating a copy of town buildings, small scale houses and the beautiful centuries' old market square. They included a detailed replica of the magnificent 1352 Cathedral of Our Lady, one of the finest gothic buildings in Europe. Perhaps the exquisite carvings are a long cry from the utilitarian history of block ice, but it's not so far from the painted wagons and colorful signs announcing the relief and joy of having some ice in your life.

CRAZY NEW CUSTOMERS

First, there was regular old ice, lots and lots of it during the Ice Age from two million to 11,000 years ago. Bringing ice from the outdoors to the indoors, the natural ice trade turned ice into a highly coveted commodity for countries around the globe. Manufactured ice then removed our reliance on Mother Nature altogether. Now, in a twist of fate, manufactured blocks of ice are being employed to create an artificial outdoor ice environment—for polar bears, of course. The Arctic Ring of Life at the Detroit Zoo in Michigan houses seven very cold, very happily cold polar bears by using ice machines that make gigantic 1,800-pound blocks of ice. At 4.2 acres, the installation is the world's largest polar bear exhibit. It is also the world's largest man-made ice exhibit!

In the sunny warm climate of the Florida Peninsula, a different artificial environment shows up each winter. This exhibit is for a different type of animal—gadabout tourists. Gaylord Palms Resort, in Orlando, uses two million pounds of crystal clear block ice to give tourists the most beautiful, colorful and cold Christmas Florida has ever known. The blocks are carved into a full-size horse and sleigh, crystal clear tin soldiers, beautiful bunnies and fawns, and a complete nativity scene. They even offer an ice castle slide to zoom down—if tourists have warm enough clothes to protect against the nine-degree-Fahrenheit temperature. To add color, many of the sculptures in the 18,000-square-foot exhibit have lights inside, "creating an ever-changing luminescence" in a magical winter wonderland.

Block ice is used to make fancy bars for corporate parties, keeping the vodka at the perfect temperature. It's used for making centerpieces that have logos or roses encased in the middle of an ice ball. It's marketed for wedding receptions as an "ice luge," a block of ice with either a simple channel cut through the middle where the bartender pours the liquid for instant chilling or with a copper tube placed in during the freezing process so the drinks are chilled but not watered down. There's an ice hotel in the arctic circle

of Lapland in Sweden that uses ice from the adjoining river to make clear chairs, clear beds and clear tables. I'm certain the trend will take off in areas not lucky enough to have all the required construction material underfoot. Manufactured block ice may be the groundwork for your four-poster bed the next time you check into an avant-garde Las Vegas hotel.

One of the new trends in ice across the country, both for block ice and for the more common fragmentary ice, is overland transportation. In the past, icemen would lose too much of the product if it traveled a long distance. Protected now by refrigerated trailers in an eighteen-wheeler rig, the 144 blocks, or 42,200 pounds, of ice stay frozen solid until distributed to concrete companies, caterers and ice plants that size the ice into twelve-pound blocks for resale. Adel Ice Company, in Adel, Georgia, still makes block ice in their 1927 plant but now ships the 300-pounders to cities down in south Florida and all the way up to Michigan, 1000 miles away. L. L. "Buddy" Duke, III, grandson of the original owner, Lloyd Duke, Sr., ships his ice for produce use in the summer and for snow at playtime activities in the winter months of December, January and February. The original plant produced approximately 108 blocks a day but third-generation iceman Mr. Duke now produces 650 blocks of ice a day. No wonder he can transport 800 tractor-trailer loads of ice per year. This ability to chill ice during overland transportation, without one cube melting, can be extremely important after a hurricane disaster when local and nearby ice plants can't produce ice or their production cannot begin to keep up with demand. During such times, old-timers, fishermen and campers of all ages know the value of a block of ice but their numbers are dwindling. After Hurricane Ivan in 2004, one Louisiana ice plant owner tried to educate the gathering crowd of Gen-Xers that block ice was cheaper and lasted longer than fragmentary ice so it was a better buy. Unfamiliar with such a thing as block ice, they opted instead to stand in lines thirty-people-deep to wait for the more common fragmentary packaged ice. Some people say ice is ice, but block ice, as far as ice itself goes, was and still is king when it comes to the time ice lasts before it melts away.

No one knows how long block ice will be around to satisfy the prudent and whimsical cooling needs of the nation. According to the old National Ice Association, now called the International Packaged Ice Association, "Block ice plants are no longer an important factor in North America. Down-trend continues. Production used for carving cakes & packaged block (10#). However, both items are now high margin products." The very scarcity of block ice may enable block plant owners to find future customers for designer and specialty block ice products. Perhaps one day we will see crystal clear block ice become as chic as bottled water. Buying brand-name ice might seem odd but so did raising catfish in the Delta, getting folks to buy frozen foods instead of fresh, and buying man-made ice instead of what Mother Nature and God had created.

Those small ice coils on the rooftop machinery in the summer of 1845 in Apalachicola, Florida proliferated into an industry that eventually transformed an entire region and helped usher in the modern era, bringing health, happiness and comfort to all in its wake. If your air conditioning breaks down, or your refrigerator goes on the blink, or you taste the succulent sweetness of a strawberry on the shores of Lake Michigan, think about block ice and the men and women of that era who experienced artificial coolness for the very first time. Block ice, once a preeminent industry, faded out of the spotlight without much ceremony until it is now just a shell of its old self. Even though there are only about sixty or seventy block ice plants left in the United States, over half of them in Southern states with our long, heat-sustaining summers, one thing is certain: the block ice industry deserves our indebtedness, commendation, and esteem for a job well done.

So here's to all of you who are keeping the torch alive with the sweat of your brow in a labor-intensive, backbreaking business. Here's to all of you who are amassing tools of the trade and preserving the history of the industry in museums. Cheers to each of you for offering future generations the chance to know the labor of our ancestors who brought coolness and comfort to Americans during the most mechanically progressive era that the world will ever know. Be cool.

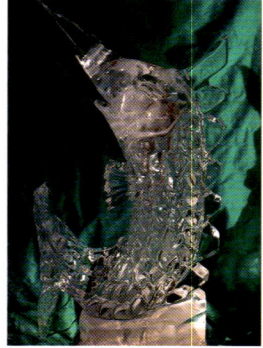

Chandler Echols, ice carver, Savannah, Georgia.

FROZEN ASSETS

BIBLIOGRAPHY

Alexander, Clay. Interview by author. Jackson, MS, 10 Aug. 2003.

Alexander, Dean. Interview by author. Jackson, MS, 17 Aug. 2003.

Alexander, Jane. Interview by author. Jackson, MS, 07 Aug. 2003.

"All About Ice—The Way Ahead!" *All About Ice*. 7 June-July 2007 <http://www.allaboutice.com>.

Anderson, Jr., Oscar E. *Refrigeration in America*. Princeton: Princeton UP, 1953.

"Arctic Ring of Life." Detroit Zoo. 20 Feb. 2005 <http://www.detroitzoo.org/Attractions/ARL/Arctic_Ring_of_Life/>.

Arenz, Kathrine. Interview by author. Friar's Point, MS, 14 Apr. 2004.

Baker, C. T. "Observations The Year 1960." *Refrigeration* 113.1 (1961): 2+.

Barr, James. Interview by author. Oxford, MS, 25 Aug. 2003.

Barthe, Kathy. Interview by author. West Chester, PA, 23 Feb. 2004.

Becker, Raymond B. *John Gorrie, M. D.: Father of Air Conditioning and Mechanical Refrigeration*. New York: Carlton P, 1972. 104-194.

Behmke, Mildred. Interview by author. Mexico Beach, FL, 22 Apr. 2005.

Bridges, Charles. Interview by author. Jackson, MS, 21 Aug. 2003.

Brown, Billy Ross. Interview by author. Oxford, MS, 24 Aug. 2003.

Brown, Billy Ross. Telephone interview by author. 23 Aug. 2003.

Bush, David. Interview by author. Savannah, GA, 24 Feb. 2004.

Carter, George Duey. Interview by author. Pascagoula, MS, 15 Aug. 2003.

Cobb, Georgie Simms. Interview by author. Canton, MS, 6 Aug. 2003.

Creekmore, Judy. "Reserve Food Firm's History Is Recalled." *The Picayune* 27 Mar. 2005, sec. I: 1-2.

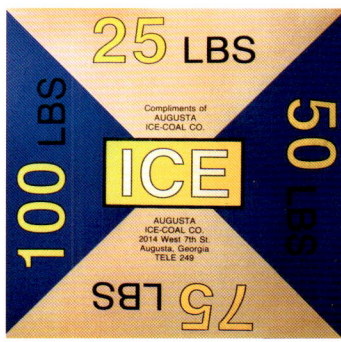

Cristina, Robert. "History of Ice Manufacturing—Cristina Family." Unpublished family history in possession of author.

Cristina, Kenny. Interview by author. Marrero, LA, 16 Nov. 2004.

Cristina, Robert J. Interview by author. Harahan, LA, 16 Nov. 2004.

Cronley, Joe. "Why We Did a Millennium Issue." *Refrigeration* 183.1 (2001): 5.

Cronley, Mary Yopp, ed. "History of Ice 1907-Today." *Refrigeration* 183.1 (2001): 24-25.

---. "1907 Sanitarium." *Refrigeration* 183.1 (2001): 9.

Davis, Rob. Personal interview. 9 Oct. 2006.

De Veronica, Joey. Interview by author. Gulfport, MS, 15 Aug. 2003.

"Disaster Ice." *International Packaged Ice Association*. 14 Mar. 2004 <http://www.packagedice.org/>.

"Disastrous Fire Destroys Two Largest Factories On Banks of Pearl." Jackson Daily News 9 Nov. 1923.

Duke, Buddy. Telephone interview. 9 July 2007.

Chapel, George L. "Dr. John Gorrie Refrigeration Pioneer." Apalachicola, Fl: Apalachicola Area Historical Society, Inc.

"Eppy". Interview by author. Pascagoula, MS, 15 Aug. 2003.

Fargason, Jim. Interview by author. Jackson, MS, 14 Apr. 2004.

Farrell, Mary. "Oxford Ice Man Solid in Tradition." *Oxford Eagle* 30 Sept. 1985, sec. Living: 1.

Falkner, Lamar. "Oldest Firm Dates to Ice by Boat." *Jackson Daily News* 5 June 1955.

Fortner, Chris. Interview by author. Cairo, GA, 11 Nov. 2004.

Fortner, Jr., W. C. "Sonny". Interview by author. Anguilla, MS, 10 Aug. 2003.

"Frick History." Frick. 14 Mar. 2004 <http://www.frickcold.com/dynapage.asp?TopicDisplay=20&PageView=ON&PageDisplay=ON&PageMasterDisplay=ON&cnt_WebPage_ID=35>.

Fulgham, Ben. Interview by author. Jackson, MS, 21 Aug. 2003.

Gautier, David. Interview by author. Pascagoula, MS, 15-16; 20 Aug. 2003.

Gorrie, John. United States. United States Patent Office. *Improved Process for the Artificial Production of Ice*. Washington: United States Patent Office, 1851.

Green, Baird. Telephone interview by author. 21 Oct. 2004.

Harris, Wendy E., and Arnold Pickman. "Slip—Slidin' Away: Archaeology and the Reconstruction of the Hudson River Ice Industry." Oct. 1998. Council For Northeast Historical Archaeology. 7 July 2007 <http://members.aol.com/cragscons2/cneha98.htm>.

Circa 1925 J. Chein tin replica of a 1928 Mac AC ice wagon.

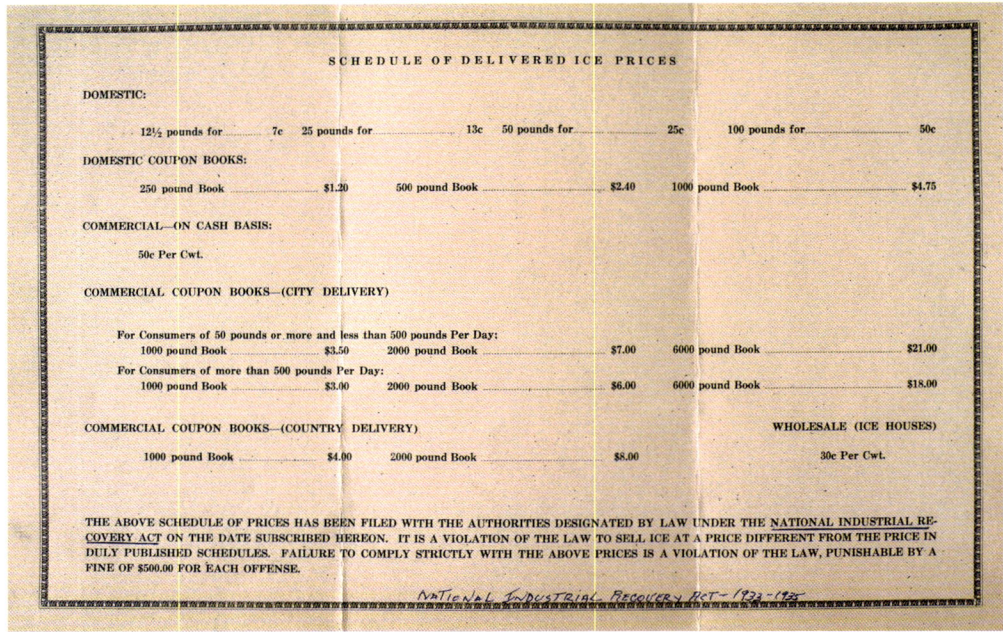

Pricing structure instituted by National Industrial Recovery Act. Ruled unconstitutional in 1935.

Hartin, Don. Interview by author. Mexico Beach, FL, 28 Jan. 2005.

Hayden, Robert C. *9 African American Inventors*. New York: 21st Century Books, 1992. 46-61.

Hembel, Jeff. "Ask the Antiques Expert." *Country Woman* Sept.-Oct. 1990: 64.

Hildebrandt, David. Interview by author. Cairo, GA, 11 Nov. 2004.

Hill, Dewey D., and Elliott R. Hughes. *Ice Harvesting in Early America*. New Hartford: New Hartford Historical Society, 1977. 35-41.

Hirshberg, Dr., Leonard Keene. "The Value of Ice." *Refrigeration* 27.2 (1920): 22.

Historical Home Tour. Manship House, Jackson, Ms. 13 Aug. 2003.

"History." Vilter. 14 Mar. 2004 <http://www.vilter.com/history.html>.

Holley, Brandi. Interview by author. Oxford, MS, 24 Aug. 2003.

"How City Products Ice Is Manufactured." Advertisement. *St. Louis Globe-Democrat* 24 May 1953.

"Hurricane Camille's Victims Cue Up for Iceman's Ice; Plants Serve Severe Demand with Adequate Supply." *Refrigeration* 130.3 (1969): 1.

"HVAC Time Line." *SSAW Home Services Company*. 6 June 2004 <http://www.ssaw-services.com/rses/timeline.html>.

"Ice—and the June Bride." Advertisement. *Refrigeration* 183.1 (2001):34. Originally published in *Refrigeration* 45.4 (1929).

"Ice Plant Directory Delta States Ice Association." Delta States Ice Association, 1964.

"Ice Plant Unchanged Since 1935; Owner, Tanks, Equipment Are Same." *Refrigeration* 128.3 (1968): 1.

"It Pays to Ice the Year 'Round." Advertisement. *Ladies Home Journal* Sept. 1928.

"Jackson Landmarks." Jackson, Ms: Junior League of Jackson, 1982.

Jacobs, Paul E. Letter to the author. 8 Feb. 2005.

Jenkins, M A., ed. "Morris Ice Company Mississippi Pioneer." *Refrigeration* 114.1 (1961): 1+.

"John Gorrie State Museum." Florida State Parks. 4 Mar. 2004 <http://www.abfla.com/parks/JohnGorrie/johngorrie.html>.

Jones, Bertha. Interview by author. Canton, MS, 6 Aug. 2003.

Jones, Jr., Joseph C. *America's Icemen An Illustrative History of the United States Natural Ice Industry 1665-1925*. Humble: Jobeco Books, 1984. 13-14, 137-155.

Krasner-Khait, Barbara. "The Impact of Refrigeration." *History Magazine*. 14 Mar. 2004 <http://www.history-magazine.com/refrig.html>.

Krieder, Janice E. "Memories On Ice." *Michigan Natural Resources* Nov.-Dec. 1998: 19-22.

Lacey, James H. Telephone interview by author. 6 Aug. 2003.

LaPlante, Helen. Interview by author. Mexico Beach, FL, 22 Apr. 2005.

Lindsay, Arnold. "Alert Aids Bottlers, Hurts Eateries." *The Clarion-Ledger* 23 July 2003, sec. C: 1+.

Major, G. F. "Ice Sawing Device." *Refrigeration* 27.2 (1920): 29.

"Manship House Museum." Jackson, Ms: Ms Department of Archives and History.

McCormick, J. "Raw Water Ice." *Refrigeration* 27.2 (1920): 23+.

McIntyre, Charlie. Telephone interview by author. 15 Nov. 2003.

Mississippi. Bureau of Census. *Ice Plants 1934-35, Study of Ad Valorem Assessments in Various Mississippi Industries*. Jackson: Bureau of Census, 1935.

Mitchell, Terry. "Community Refrigeration Centers Meet Public Service Demands." *Refrigeration* 91.5 (1950): 3.

Moffatt, Matt. "History of Ice Manufacturing At the Turn

of the 20th Century." *Ice Manufacture*. University of Maryland. 23 June 2003 <http://www.otal.umd.edu/~vg/amst205.F97/vj12/project5.html>.

Montz, Gerard. "Hello Ms. Morris." Email to the author. 15 Dec. 2004.

---. "Hello Ms. Morris." Email to the author. 27 Apr. 2005.

---. Letter to the author. 11 Apr. 2005.

Moore, John Hebron. Telephone interview by author. 09 Oct. 2004.

Morris, Hebron. Letter to the author. 08 June 2003.

---. Letter to the author. 22 July 2003.

---. Letter to the author. 27 July 2003.

---. Letter to the author. 31 Oct. 2004.

---. Letter to the author. 17 May 2005.

--- Interview by author. Jackson, MS, 1-23 Aug. 2003.

Nagengast, Bernard. "It's a Cool Story!" *Mechanical Engineering Magazine Online*. American Society of Mechanical Engineers. 14 Mar. 2004 <http://www.memagazine.org/backissues/may00/features/coolstory/coolstory.html.

"National Ice Carving Association." *National Ice Carving Association*. 17 May 2005 <http://www.nica.org/>.

"National Industrial Recovery Act." *Wikipedia*. 1 Nov. 2004 <http://en.wikipedia.org/wik/National_Industrial_Recovery_Act>.

Neal, Rob. Interview by author. Savannah, GA, 24 Feb. 2004.

"New Publications." *Cornell Making of America*. Cornell University Library. 23 June 2003 <http://cdl.library.cornell.edu/cgi-bin/moa/pageviewer?frames=1&coll=moa&view=50&root=%2Fmoa%2Fmanu%2Fmanu0011%2F&tif=00268.TIF&cite=http%3A%2F%2Fcdl.library.cornell.edu%2Fcgi-bin%2Fmoa%2Fmoa-cgi%3Fnotisid%3DABS1821-0011-735>.

Nolan, Mary. Interview by author. Mexico Beach, FL, 22 Apr. 2005.

Norton, Roy. Interview by author. Port St. Joe, FL, 19 Feb. 2005.

Norvell, H. D. "Ice Men of the Nation." National Association of Ice Industries. Annual Convention, National Association of Ice Industries. St. Louis. 5 Oct. 1920 in *Refrigeration* 27.3 (1920): 22-25.

"Old Ammonia Block Ice Plants Still Operating in the USA as of July 2002." Chart. Philadelphia: Ice Plant Equipment Co., Inc., 2002.

Oliver, S. C. Address. Southern Ice Exchange. Southern Ice Exchange Convention. New Orleans. 27 Nov. 1922 in *Refrigeration* 31.5 (1922): 34.

"Pelican Ice Company." *Nutrias*. New Orleans Public Library. 14 Mar. 2004 <http://nutrias.org/~nopl/monthly/mar2002/pelican.htm>.

Peters, Anderson. Interview by author. Pascagoula, MS, 20 Aug. 2003.

Polk, Tommy. Interview by author. Clarksdale, MS, 13 Apr. 2004.

"Pops". Interview by author. Richmond, VA, 26 May 2003.

Post, Jr., James B. "Exit the Iceman—Enter Friqus Agua." National Ice Association. National Ice Association Convention. Wilkes-Barre, PA in *Refrigeration* 113.3 (1961): 1+.

Principal Ice Producing and Distributing Companies in the United States. National Ice Association. Washington, Dc: National Ice Association, 1965. 46-48.

Quinlivan, Steve. Interview by author. Mobile, AL, 18 Nov. 2004.

"Refrigeration." *The Handbook of Texas Online*. Texas State Historical Association and University of Texas. 14 Mar. 2004 <http://www.tsha.utexas.edu/handbook/online/articles/RR/dqr1.html>.

"Refrigerator." *Idea Finder*. 20 Oct. 2004 <http://www.ideafinder.com/history/inventions/story057.htm>.

Reinke, Debby. Interview by author. Prospect, VA, 27 Nov. 2003.

Reynolds, Hal, ed. "The Automatic Plant." *Refrigeration* 46.7 (1930): 48.

---. "Frozen Products." *Refrigeration* 46.7 (1930): 49.

---. "They Want to Know." *Refrigeration* 46.7 (1930): 47-48.

---. "What Do You Know?" *Refrigeration* 46.7 (1930): 44.

Ribeiro, Sr., Walter G. "The Ice Industry in South Jersey," parts 1, 2, and 3, *South Jersey Magazine* Fall 1994: 16-21; Winter 2005: 10-15; Spring 1995: 16-21.

(left) Circa 1930 5x5 ammonia compressor, Scott's Ice Company;
(middle) 1946 safe, M&M Ice and Cold Storage;
(right) Insulation in between walls of ice storage room, Triangle Ice Company.

---. "Evolution of the "Ice Cube"" *South Jersey Magazine* Fall 1997: 33-36.

---. Letter to the author. 18 Sept. 2004.

---. Letter to the author. 18 Oct. 2004.

---. Letter to the author. 05 Nov. 2004.

---. Letter to the author. 21 Jan. 2005.

---. Interview by author. West Chester, PA, 20 Feb. 2004.

Robertson, Jr., Louis. Interview by author. Kenner, LA, 15 Nov. 2004.

Romig, David. Interview by author. Kenner and Marrero, LA, 15-16 Nov. 2004.

Sandifer, Nathaniel. Interview by author. Jackson, MS, 10 Aug. 2003.

Schleh, Clara. Interview by author. Long Beach, MS, 14 Aug. 2003.

Shapiro, Ron. Interview by author. Oxford, MS, 23 Aug. 2003.

Sherlock, V M. *The Fever Man: a Biography of Dr. John Gorrie*. St. Charles: Medallion P, 1982.

"Significant Milestones in Illinois Central Railroad History." *Illinois Central Historical Society*. 20 Oct. 2004 <http://icrrhistorical.org/milestones.html>.

Smith, Michael. Interview by author. Cairo, GA, 11 Nov. 2004.

Stack, Pete. Interview by author. West Chester, PA, 20 Feb. 2004.

Starkes, Willy. Interview by author. Clarksdale, MS, 13 Apr. 2004.

"Statement of Significance for Kramertown-Railroad Historic District Nomination." Mississippi Department of Archives and History,1980. Originally published by Hancock, Jack. "Spotlight on McComb—a City That Was Built on Purpose." *Jackson, [Miss.] Daily News* 31 July 1949.

Stevens, Rose Budd. *From Rose Budd's Kitchen*. Jackson and London: University Press of Mississippi, 1988.

Talbott, George M. *Vegetables On Ice*. Florida Ice Association, Nov. 1960 in *Refrigeration* 113.1 (1961): 1+.

"The McComb Ice House and Creamery Timeline," Plague on wall of The Ice House, McComb, MS.

"The People's Vote." *U.S. News & World Report*. 1 Nov. 2004 <http://www.usnews.com/usnews/home.htm>.

"The Story of Convenience Shopping." 7-Eleven. 12

Flywheel of Bruce McBeth natural gas engine, MICO.

Oct. 2003 <http://www.7-eleven.com/about/history.asp>.

Ulm, Aaron Hardy. "The Truth About Cold Storage." *Refrigeration* 27.2 (1920): 26-28.

Utley, R S., ed. "Delta States Ice Association Holds Silver Anniversary Meet." *Refrigeration* 113.3 (1961): 1+.

Vandeness, Lynn. Interview by author. Richmond, VA, 05 May 2003.

---. Interview by author. Richmond, VA, 30 Sept. 2005.

Van Hecke, Merwin. Telephone interview by author. 30 Sept. 2003.

"Vogt Ice History." *Vogt Ice, LLC*. 14 Mar. 2004 <http://www.vogtice.com/>.

Wacker, Charles C. "Ice Wagons & Trucks." *Double Clutch* May-June 2004: 35-37.

Watson, Charlie. Interview by author. Tupelo, MS, 25 Aug. 2003.

Weaver, Jim. "Information You Requested." Email to the author. 18 Nov. 2005.

Weightman, Gavin. *The Frozen Water Trade: a True Story*. New York: Hyperion, 2003. 210-244.

"What Is the SIE." *Southern Ice Exchange*. 2 Nov. 2003 <http://www.sietoday.com/new_page_2.htm>.

Wilkinson, Bill. Interview by author. Constitution Convention Museum, Port St. Joe, FL, 10 Feb. 2005.

Willoughby, O. J., ed. "1950 Ice Sales 33,897,798 Tons—Drop of 18 Per Cent Over Previous Year. Sized Ice Sales Also Drop." *Refrigeration* 94.2 (1952): 1-2.

---. "Hydro-Cooling, Stericooling Improves Peach Taste, Value." *Refrigeration* 91.6 (1950): 1-2.

---. "National Advertising of Swift Iced Poultry Starts in April." *Refrigeration* 91.6 (1950): 1.

---. "Retards Camellia Blooming by Use of Crushed Ice." *Refrigeration* 91.6 (1950): 1.

---. "Sad? Maybe Not!" *Refrigeration* 94.11 (1951): 2.

---. "Super-Cooled Club Pool Offers New Ice Market." *Refrigeration* 94.2 (1952): 2.

---. "Transport Icing." *Refrigeration* 91.5 (1950): 4.

Woolrich, W. R. *The Men Who Created Cold: a History of Refrigeration*. New York: Exposition P, 1967. 13-14; 137-159.

Yopp, Jr., John W., ed. "Ice Plant Makes Possible Snowball Fight At University of Georgia." *Refrigeration* 130.3 (1969): 1.

Yopp, Sr., John W., ed. "Humanizing the Ice Business." *Refrigeration* 26.4 (1920): 21-210.

---. "Development of Refrigerating Industry in the South." *Refrigeration* 27.1 (1920): 36.

---. "Ice Prices Compared to Other Commodities." *Refrigeration* 31.5 (1922): 40.

"All In"
A PEERLESS Head Protector
Could Save Him
It's Ammonia Proof. **Order Now**

THE VINTON COMPANY
Home Life Building   NEW YORK

TO PROVIDE YOUR DRIVERS WITH

ICE TOOLS

OF QUALITY, IS SIMPLY A GOOD
BUSINESS INVESTMENT—SEND FOR CATALOGUE

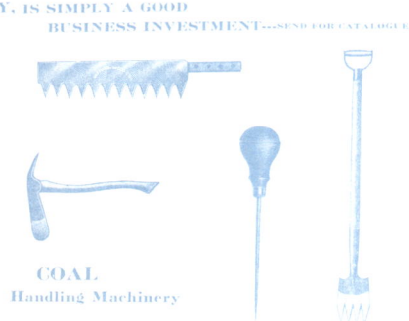

COAL
Handling Machinery

Gig Elevator and Lowering Machine.

This equipment designed for loading and lowering ice in and out of storage.

Built to handle one or more cakes simultaneously.

Automatic Lowering Machine.

Constructed entirely of steel. Entirely automatic in its operation. Handles cakes gently and without breakage.

WRITE FOR PRICES ON EQUIPMENT
COVERING YOUR REQUIREMENTS

Gifford Wood Co.
HUDSON, N.Y.   CHICAGO, ILL.

freezing and agitation
...divisions.
...sed or tried three different...nection with this system...sh much difference in...thickness of ice. First...tween the oblong sides...ce for the cans. Next...in a brine solution...ammonia coil and put...and under each can

Wet-Strength Paper Ice Bags
have tremendous strength even when soaking wet...thanks to a water repellent resin that binds the fibres of the paper firmly together.

Iced Tea Time

51 JULY 1951

1	2	3	4	5	6	7
8	9					
15						
22	23					
29	30	31				

NATIONAL ICED TEA TIME
JULY 13-20

National Iced Tea Time will be celebrated from July 13th to the 20th. The Iced Tea Queen for the summer of 1951 will be chosen in St. Louis, where iced tea was discovered in 1904. Mary Collins, a Conover model (above) wants to remind you that iced tea is an all-summer-long favorite. Copies of this photograph and other publicity material for Iced Tea Time can be obtained by ice companies for use in their local papers from the Tea Bureau, Inc., 150 Fifth Ave., New York 11.

DePrez Manufacturing Company
Purchased By Lusk Corporation

the size may be different...but the result will be the same!

ICE MEN! WATCH FOR THE GREAT NEWS FROM PERFECTION ICE SCORING MACHINE CO.

SHOWING TRANSPARENCY AND COMPARATIVE REGULARITY IN SHAPE OF BLOCK.

...ese cans are "nested"
...necessary waste brine
...nd these cans through
...overflowing out near
...brine had been pre-
...in a tank or double

permanent tank we propose to use seamless steel cans, which would make them practically indestructible, the sides and bottom being formed out of one plate at the mill, and the small ends being brazed in by the oxygen process. A space of only one to two inches is allowed between the cans and between the cans and the tank for the...

As Different as NIGHT AND DAY!
For Complete Ice Service, Call...
PEOPLE'S ICE COMPANY
SYRACUSE — 1014 OSWEGO BLVD.

We say ice should be seen... ...not hid

...inter... With Sunny Skies and Summer Temperature

BONART
Rubel
For Ice UNIFORMS
New Price $3.75

Bonart Uniforms, Inc.

"CHILLY BILLY" MAKES TELEVISION DEBUT

CHILLY BILLY

Federal REFRIGERATOR MFG. CO.
WAUKESHA · WISCONSIN

---

* smart appearance
* efficient operation

THE PROGRESS
Icetemp No. 471

Place Your Order
NOW!

Progress
REFRIGERATOR COMPANY

Congressman John R. Anderson, Illinois, has before the Congress a bill which would amend the law to provide that only firms with a volume of $500,000 should be subject to the law.

Submitted to a nationwide vote by the National Federation of Independent Business, the results showed...per cent in favor, 22 per cent opposed, with 6 per cent undecided.

DEVELOPMENT OF CRYOGENICS

There is a relatively new development in heat dissipating that makes the refrigerator's liquid temperature seem positively balmy.

It is called cryogenics, the science of super-cold temperatures.

The average temperature of a refrigerator's freezing compartment ranges between...al 5 degrees Fahrenheit, cool enough to freeze a juicy leg of lamb into a rock hard club. But the temperatures...

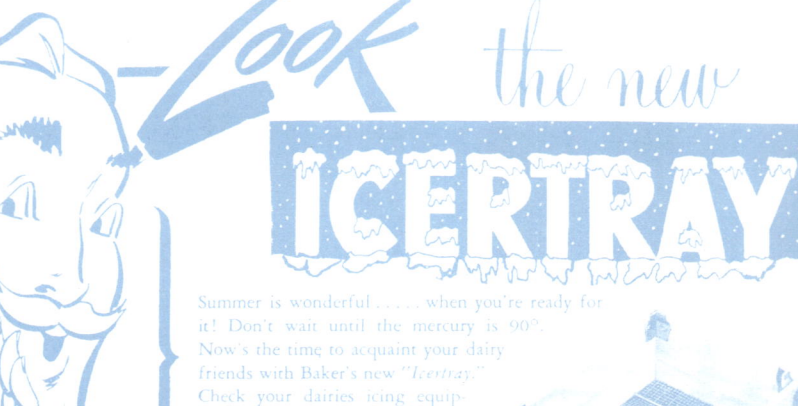

Look the new ICERTRAY

Summer is wonderful...when you're ready for it! Don't wait until the mercury is 90°. Now's the time to acquaint your dairy friends with Baker's new *"Icertray."* Check your dairies icing equipment and show them that when the *"Icertray"* is filled with crushed ice and placed on a stack of milk cases in the truck, it will improve cooling, handling and sanitation of the milk. Then you can sit back and relax being assured that your dairy is well protected this summer.

Write for *Free* literature on Baker's new *"Icertray"* that will help increase your profits!

Save Costs!
Increase Profits!

BAKER BOX
A DIVISION OF CONNOHIO, INC.
161 UNION STREET   WORCESTER 8, MASS.